Threat Perception in International Crisis

Threat Perception in International Crisis

RAYMOND COHEN

The University of Wisconsin Press

Published 1979
The University of Wisconsin Press
114 North Murray Street
Madison, Wisconsin 53715

The University of Wisconsin Press, Ltd.
1 Gower Street
London WC1E 6HA, England

First printing
Printed in the United States of America

For LC CIP information see the colophon
ISBN 0–299–08000–5

To my wife, Rivka

Contents

Part I
Introduction

Chapter 1

Threat Perception

Research in international crisis takes it for granted that a perception of threat is central to the overall phenomenon. Indeed, Charles Hermann cites the threat to "high-priority goals of the decision-making unit" as one of the three defining characteristics of international crisis.[1] Michael Brecher, Glenn Snyder, and Paul Diesing are only the latest to accept this widely held assumption.[2] It is hard to fault this view, and I would even wish to suggest that threat perception is, if anything, the decisive intervening variable between event and reaction in international crisis. For when threat is not perceived, even in the face of apparently objective evidence, there can hardly be a mobilization of defensive resources. Hence surprise. Conversely, as Klaus Knorr points out, threat may be perceived—and countermeasures taken—even when the supposed opponent possesses no malicious intent.[3]

Thus, a systematic and detailed analysis of threat perception is of no small importance, I believe, in contributing both to our understanding of international crisis in particular and of international politics in general. In this project I set out empirically to investigate the perception of threat in international crisis on the basis of a comparative analysis of historical case studies. My aim is to provide a description of the phenomenon and the conditions under which it occurs, and an explanation for its occurrence which can be accommodated within some overall conception of the subject. The former is a necessary prelude to the latter.

Threat, of course, has two quite separate meanings. The first sense is of a communication or undertaking by one actor to impose a sanction on another. The *Random House Dictionary of the English Language* defines *threat* as the "declaration of or intention to inflict punishment, injury, death or [at least] loss upon someone in retaliation for, or conditionally upon, some action or course."[4] In this study we shall understand *threat* in the altogether different sense of a perception of danger—as David Baldwin puts it, as a passive "outcome" rather than as an active "undertaking."[5] This distinction is of the essence. Charles Lockhart is quite right to argue that "those who scrutinize undertakings and perceptions of harm respectively are simply dealing with different phenomena."[6]

A perception of threat, therefore, should be understood here as an anticipation on the part of an observer, the decisionmaker, of impending harm—usually of a military, strategic, or economic kind—to the state. At this stage I shall avoid specifying either the minimal degree of expected harm required to shift the observer over the threshold of threat perception or precisely what objectives, values, or anticipated outcomes are felt to be at stake. These are questions for empirical investigation. Further, the event or series of events which give rise to the anticipation of future harm may or may not have been deliberately communicated and may consist of an act, an articulation, or some combination of both. Again, the precise nature of the threatening signs is open to investigation, but I do, *prima facie*, accept Klaus Knorr's view that perceived threats can be either "actual," that is, inferred from more or less definite signals of intent, or "potential," that is, inferred from some state of the environment or the mere capability of the opponent.[7]

To summarize, I am not interested in the sort of questions strategists have posed—for instance, when threats possess credibility—but rather in the circumstances or conditions that lead a decisionmaker to interpret a configuration in the external environment as a warning of future danger. This study is an attempt to account for a particular category of perceptions.

The literature on threat perception in international politics has been very much influenced by a relatively early theoretical discussion of the topic by David Singer. Threat, according to his estimation,

> arises out of a situation of armed hostility, in which each body of policy-makers assumes that the other entertains aggressive designs; further, each assumes that such designs will be pursued by physical and direct means if estimated gains seem to outweigh estimated losses. Each perceives the other as a threat to its national security, and such perception is a function of both estimated capability and estimated intent. To state the relationship in quasi-mathematical form: Threat-Perception = Estimated Capability × Estimated Intent.

Central to Singer's argument is the belief that "a powerful predisposition to suspect and distrust the people and government of all other nation-states" underlies the perceptions of decisionmakers: "A combination of recent events, historical memory, and identifiable sociocultural differences provides the vehicle by which this vague out-group suspicion may be readily converted into concrete hostility toward a specific foreign power."[8]

The primary problem with the Singer account is a blurring of the distinction between prescriptive and descriptive aspects of the concept. Strategic analysts do indeed, as a point of methodology, tend to organize their assessments of potential opponents on the basis of a helpful analytical distinction between capabilities and intentions.[9] Their task is scientifically to evaluate whether or not there is a danger of enemy attack—to engage in *threat analysis*. But this is far from implying that *as a matter of fact* an actual *perception* of threat will be based on any such measured calculation. Singer surely overlooks the irrational and involuntary aspect of threat perception. There is a crucial gap between a cold, scientific conclusion that a given opponent possesses a particular capability and may well possess a certain intent—the intelligence evaluation of the existence of a possible threat—and the essentially subjective conviction—the "gut feeling"—that one is in danger.

There is no reason to believe that "capability" and "intent" uniquely determine a perception of threat, as is implied by the Singer equation. This perception seems to require something else, at a different level of appraisal, to trigger the warning response. In fact, intelligence experts are no less human in this than their political masters, the people whose subjective judgment counts, and even their "scientific" estimate is as likely to be the product of intuitive conviction as of pure reason. Clearly the Singer account fails to consider the psychological dimension.

Defining threat perception as "the expectation that another nation will be harmful *in a specific way*"—that is, will endanger "a basic goal"—Dean Pruitt develops Singer's initial theoretical formulation. Threat perception, he argues, involves an *inference* rather than the "perception of something tangible." Evidence of two kinds (here Pruitt follows Singer precisely), "of capability to do harm and . . . of intent to do it," is pieced together by the observer into a coherent picture. But this "piecing together," the psychology of inference suggests to Pruitt, is not a wholly objective process, since it is partly based "on *predispositions* that affect the interpretation of evidence." Two generalizations are introduced: "(*a*) The stronger a predisposition, the more influence it will have on what is inferred. (*b*) The weaker or more ambiguous the evidence, the greater the influence of predispositions." Predispositions to perceive threat are derived from such sources as distrust, past experience, contingency planning, and personal anxiety. These may "create systematic distortions in the perception of evidence, leading to 'possibilistic thinking' in which future events are seen as probable that should only be seen as possible." Without enlarging on "evidence of capability," Pruitt orders "evidence of intent" under the following heads: (1) *Capability:* armament may in itself give rise to suspicion. (2) *Actions:* "When intentions are inferred from actions, the actions are being used as *signs.*" The most important sign "from which an intention is inferred consists of *stepping over* a 'boundary' on a conceptual dimension" (here Pruitt follows an idea of Schelling).[10] Signs are often interpreted in a particular way because of past experience; hence, (3) *Statements:* "When predispositions are strong, even minor statements may look like evidence of threat." (4) *Conditions faced by the other nation:* "The more benefit a nation can derive from harming our interests, the more threatened we are likely to feel."[11] Thus, within the basic framework suggested by Singer (predisposition/capability/ intention), Pruitt provides a coherent and self-consistent formulation.

The main difficulty with the Pruitt thesis, shared with that of Singer, is that while helpful conceptual distinctions are made, no adequate explanation is ultimately provided of why threat is perceived. The capability/intention equation is a tautology, in that all evidence can be defined to fit into either of these two categories, but it is not an empirical description of what actually takes place in the psychological process.

There is, clearly, a limit to the usefulness of purely theoretical studies in a particular subject. A point is reached at which empirical research has to take over. Unfortunately until very recently research into threat perception as a historical phenomenon tended to be minimal. Consideration of the topic can be found in some of the "Stanford" content analysis studies of the 1960s, but it is treated as an independent rather than a dependent variable; that is, it is accepted as given and its role in some aspect of state behavior analyzed.[12] In a simulation about the spread of nuclear weapons, Richard Brody and others seek to confirm the Singer formulation that "intent plus capability is related to threat perception." While the report of this simulation is not always clear, it seems that the indicators used to represent the two variables were "1) the transmission of communication [*sic*] containing hostile themes and 2) the production of military capability." In their theoretical model the researchers are at great pains to avoid oversimplification and to take into account the internal nature of the actor. Unfortunately they find themselves unable to operationalize this more complex model and are forced to work with the less satisfactory unmediated stimulus-response model. They accept its predictive power as "relatively weak" but hope that the resultant correlations will be significant. The restricted and tendentious character of the operational model and of the variables fed into it (formulated expressly with the Singer equation in mind) scarcely allow one to draw any conclusions about threat perception in the real world.[13]

Only recently have students of international politics begun to take an empirical interest in threat perception as a dependent variable. Charles Lockhart, writing in 1973, studied the efficacy of threats in the 1911 Agadir Crisis. Although primarily concerned with threat as an active undertaking, he does, to his credit, pay attention to the reciprocal factor of perception—or, more precisely, misperception—in the strategic interaction. His principal conclusion in this respect is that domestic political pressures can have an important influence on decisionmakers' receptivity to threat. French Prime Minister Caillaux, for instance, came under intense pressure from chauvinist groups to fall in line with their alarmist appraisal of German actions and paid for his efforts at rapprochement with Germany through the fall of his cabinet. In Germany Foreign Minister Kiderlen-Waechter also came under domestic pressure but, ensured of the support of the kaiser, enjoyed a greater degree of latitude.[14] Here, surely, is a factor overlooked in purely theoretical studies, which will deserve further attention.

The latest empirical study of threat perception—and by far the most important to date—is that of Klaus Knorr.[15] He is the first to seek to explain the topic by analyzing a wide range of past examples of its occurrence. His significant innovation is in going beyond Pruitt and Singer to draw attention to the actual cognitive process of threat perception. Realizing, from the example of the periods preceding the two World Wars, that threat may or may not be perceived, irrespective of the objective condition of the external environment, Knorr concludes that although threat is derived from things which in principle are observed, observable realities "rarely have unmistakable meaning"; that is, they are inherently ambiguous: "Threat perceptions rest on estimates of the past and present. These estimates are inferences from usually fragmentary, opaque and contradictory bits of information. Second, these perceptions concern the future, and there can be no reliable information about the future." Thus, threat perception is above all a "cognitive construct" which "creates an image of reality; it is a device, a hypothesis."

Given this key insight Knorr sets out to determine which factors affect the cognition—the perception of threat—of decisionmakers. Like Pruitt and Singer he discovers these in "intervening predispositions," which he categorizes into factors that lead to an underestimation of threat, facilitate the perception of threat, obstruct the perception of threat, and encourage misperception. There is some overlapping here, but the following predispositions seem to be of recurrent importance:

1. First there are the predetermined expectations and beliefs of individuals: "Facing a complex and changing real world, the peculiar mind-set of the perceiver makes attention selective." Into this category we can also include emotional factors, such as the personality of the decisionmaker, which can induce a high or low receptivity to threatening information.
2. Second is the past experience of societies, especially weak ones, Knorr argues, that have been subject to repeated attack and military pressure. Conversely, societies that are basically unfamiliar with the new opponent may disregard evidence of danger.
3. Third is the present experience of societies faced by an

opponent whose military strength is either greater or growing relative to that of the perceiver, even when that state exhibits no present indication of hostile intent.

4. Fourth are the structure and set of assumptions of the relevant bureaucracies involved in the foreign policy process. Knorr concludes that threat tends to be underestimated by governments which suffer from decentralization, inertia, and rivalry. Special interests may conflict with "objective" threat perception. Intelligence may tend to overcaution; the military may exaggerate foreign military threats in order to acquire greater budgetary resources; other bureaucracies may have the opposite interest. Finally ideological preconceptions—"more or less formalized belief systems that pretend to define reality authoritatively"—may affect perceptions of the government in whole or in part.

In addition to these explicit studies of threat perception from a political science perspective, it is also worth referring to two other essays which, though written from a historical viewpoint, do cast light on the subject. Jonathan Steinberg investigates German fears of a preventive British naval attack in the pre–World War I period:[16] "To Germans in the days of Kaiser Wilhelm II, the word 'Kopenhagen' meant more than the name of the Danish capital. It represented a past event and a present fear, the fear that some day, perhaps on a peaceful afternoon as in the autumn of 1807, a British fleet would suddenly appear off Wilhelmshaven or Kiel and without warning attack the beautiful new ships of the Imperial Navy." Tracing the roots of this fear to German pretensions of overcoming British maritime hegemony, the author then describes various concrete examples of what I have called threat perception—the fright in Germany at the time of the Dogger Bank incident of 1904, when German colliers were fueling the Russian ships which fired on British trawlers; the scare generated at the end of that year by news of an Admiralty war game, Germany versus England. In his analysis of the phenomenon—which he calls the "Copenhagen Complex"—Steinberg suggests the following explanation:

1. There was a hard core of reality to the fear. The possibility could not be entirely dismissed that the British Fleet would launch a preventive attack to protect its preponderant position.
2. There was the personal aspect. The kaiser, Steinberg argues, had a love-hate relationship with England; he admired, but also envied, England's greatness, of which her fleet was a symbol.
3. There was an element of projection. " 'Kopenhagen' really stood for a fear of what the British might do if they once found out what the Germans wanted to do."
4. There was the societal aspect. "Germany in the Wilhelmine era was an unstable society, and that instability found its expression not only in the exaggerated bombast of public life, but in the exaggerated anxieties of private reflection."

Uri Bialer, for his part, investigates the fear of air attack which pervaded British government and public circles in the period between the two World Wars and which achieved something of the status of an obsession.[17] Even before the establishment of the Luftwaffe, German air power was a constant preoccupation and was a crucial influence, Bialer demonstrates, on major decisions of foreign and defense policy. Bialer draws attention to the following elements underlying this fear:

1. There was the sense that Britain was completely open to attack from the air and that in any future war Britain's cities would be devastated. In the words of Stanley Baldwin: "The bomber will always get through." Although radar was invented in 1934–35, it was not until the very threshold of war, in 1939, that it became an operational reality that could seriously diminish the penetrative capability of an attacking force.
2. On the one hand, at the back of decisionmakers' minds was the traumatic experience of 1917, when the first daylight bombardment of London took place without any losses to the attacking force, and on the other hand was a

lack of experience since that date of large-scale air attack. (Events in Spain, Ethiopia, and China involved essentially limited efforts of strategic air bombardment.) This resulted in exaggerated estimates of the efficacy of the air weapon and an absence of up-to-date information on its time scope. No evidence was available to place air power in a more accurate perspective.

3. Finally, and more intangibly, there was an underlying philosophical assumption. The considerable advance of civil and military aviation in the interwar period, coupled with Social Darwinist ideas, suggested that a power that fell behind in the air race was doomed to inevitable defeat in the next war.

In contrast to the relative paucity of empirical material on the perception of threat in international politics, threat perception has been extensively dealt with by social psychologists in the context of studies of stress and natural disaster. One recurrent theme, for example, is the sensitivity to minimal threat cues of a community struck by catastrophes such as flood, hurricane, or earthquake.[18] Also of interest is Withey's finding that threat is more readily perceived if it conforms to a course of action to which the observer is already committed.[19] A helpful conceptual discussion and review of the material is found in Richard S. Lazarus, *Psychological Stress and the Coping Process* (New York, 1966). On the whole, though, much of this research turns out to be of only marginal significance to international relations; the situations studied—illness, combat, the Mercury space program, exposure to unpleasant stimuli in the laboratory, etc.—are only remotely analogous to actual situations in international politics. The factors relevant to man as decisionmaker, responsible for the policy of his state in the international environment, are surely different from those which are studied in more restricted social situations. This problem of relevance is accentuated when man is treated as an experimental subject, at least in the existing literature; and it is not easy to see how one might set up a laboratory experiment to simulate the threat of armed attack, with all its associated feelings of dread and horror.

Threat perception in international crisis is doubtless analogous to threat perception in everyday life. Nevertheless there are certain characteristics peculiar to international politics which suggest that one should be cautious about rigidly applying conclusions taken from the spheres of individual and social psychology. On the whole, for example, threats perceived in international crisis are to central values of the state which the decisionmaker represents, rather than to his own private interests. It is not self-evident that the same logic which applies when one's personal interests and survival are at stake will govern one's perception and judgment in the trustee role of foreign policy decisionmaker.

Moreover, whereas the kinds of threats faced by the private individual in his everyday life are invariably repetitive and typical—because millions of similar people lead similar lives in similar environments facing similar problems and challenges—this is far less true of international crisis. True, border threats and invasions are recurrent and familiar objects of international concern, and state perceptions are likely to be widely analogous. But in very many cases the threatening event or constellation of events can be found to contain wholly new elements. One may be able to discover historical precedents for the crisis, but this does not alter the likely originality of the phenomenon from the point of view of the perceiver.

Take a few examples of threat perception from recent history. In 1956, for instance, British decisionmakers perceived Nasser's nationalization of the Suez Canal as a threat. It is hard to recall even a remotely analogous event combining precisely those elements crucial in 1956: the peculiar associations of the canal for an imperial power that had only recently withdrawn troops from that area; the unfortunate resonance the dictator Nasser possessed for men who had been involved in public life at the time of Appeasement; and so on. Similarly, the Soviet blockade of Berlin in 1948 and the Soviet introduction of intercontinental missiles into Cuba in 1962 were unique events substantively different from anything that had gone before.

The task of the comparative researcher is to seek out shared aspects of ostensibly diverse examples of a given phenomenon in order to attempt to formulate some kind of covering theory. In the current investigation one point of departure must be that the threats perceived by decision-makers are likely to consist of complex and unique constellations and juxtapositions of events and circumstances. We may ultimately discover enlightening comparisons between perceived threats in international crisis and those in everyday life. But we cannot take this for granted.

The practical implication of the state of current theory and empirical findings for research into threat perception is that only a limited number of hypotheses of any plausibility are available for testing. An initial attempt of mine to examine a list of hypotheses drawn from the literature in social psychology indicated that most were neither verifiable nor refutable, but merely irrelevant to international crisis. *A priori* hypotheses based on common sense also turned out to be either irrelevant or trivial. I concluded that in the absence of a body of explanatory theory (though Pruitt, Lazarus, and Knorr provided useful conceptual frameworks), empirical research would have to be rather open-ended. The classic procedure of testing a given set of hypotheses against the empirical evidence is simply not possible. This need not be considered a unique or unsurmountable obstacle, however. Hecksher, indeed, has argued for the dispensability of hypothesizing in political science:

> On the one hand the problem has to be posed before the collection of data begins; on the other hand, hypotheses altogether without basis in fact are apt to be somewhat uninteresting. . . . Furthermore, on the basis of data collected not only our hypotheses, but even the character of our problem frequently change. There is a continual process of mutual influence between the character of the problem and the collection of the facts. Actually, while a general hypothesis is frequently inherent in the problem, what we can demand is

hardly more than that any study of the political process . . .
should start from a clearly and explicitly stated problem.[20]

Hecksher's solution to the methodological problem raised by
the need to generalize without the initial guidance of hypotheses is the comparative approach. There is no reason
why this method should not be equally applicable to international politics. The comparative analysis of historical case
studies can enable us to examine threat perception without
making any preliminary restrictive assumptions. We can pose
the question of under what conditions, and why, threat is
perceived, and then direct our attention to the common patterns—and unique aspects—displayed by our examples. Let
us proceed to examine the comparative approach in detail.

Chapter 2

The Methodology of Comparative Analysis

Almost all political analysis is comparative to some extent. As Harry Eckstein so brilliantly argues, it is rare for even the most narrowly defined single-case study to avoid all comparison, even if it is only of different stages of development of the same individual entity.[1] At the other end of the spectrum, the statistical-correlative approach, which finds its most familiar expression in the controlled experiment involving large numbers of cases thought to constitute a sample of the total population of the phenomenon in question, is also unquestionably comparative. What I mean here by comparative analysis, therefore, is what Sidney Verba calls the "disciplined configurative" approach or what Alexander George and Richard Smoke call "focused comparison"[2] —that is, an approach that examines, for a variety of reasons (lack of material, smallness of total population of examples, complexity of phenomenon), a limited number of case studies in depth within the framework of a common set of questions or merely points of reference.

The comparative approach, in the sense implied here, though early discussed by Mill,[3] is usually associated with

16

Durkheim. Comparison, he argued, performs for the social sciences the role of laboratory experimentation in the natural sciences. It obviates the necessity of excluding or even considering all possible variables, a notorious source of difficulty for the social scientist: "The mere parallelism of the series of values presented by the two phenomena, provided that it has been established in a sufficient number and variety of cases, is proof that a relationship exists between them."[4] After a lapse in popularity during the interwar period, when the method tended to be associated with discredited theories in sociology, comparative analysis began to be widely applied after the appearance in 1940 of Fortes and Evans-Pritchard's *African Political Systems*.[5] In his preface to this work Radcliffe-Brown, who is largely responsible for the revival of the approach, wrote a classic justification of comparative analysis in anthropology which can be equally applied to international politics in particular and political science in general:

> The task of social anthropology, as a natural science of human society, is the systematic investigation of the nature of social institutions. The method of natural science rests always on the comparison of observed phenomena, and the aim of such comparison is by a careful examination of diversities to discover underlying uniformities. Applied to human societies the comparative method used as an instrument for inductive inference will enable us to discover the universal, essential, characters which belong to all human societies, past, present and future.[6]

Wherever possible social scientists have, it is true, increasingly tended to prefer the statistical-correlative approach to theory-building because it eliminates randomness and subjectivity and fosters reliable, valid results. This ideal is not always attainable, however. In international politics, for instance, the researcher is frequently confronted with phenomena which are too infrequent to permit statistical manipulation or about which adequate data are available in a limited number of cases only. In this sort of research situation the comparative approach can still permit, as Neil Smelser argues, the scientific analysis of historical data.[7] A final advantage of the comparative approach in this context is suggested by George and Smoke. At the present time, they note, the statistical-correlative methodology cannot give adequate attention to the complexity and variability of the foreign policy decisionmaking process. Since intervening variables tend to alter from case to case, they cannot readily be compressed into a small number of predefined values for coding.[8]

From the fields of anthropology and sociology, comparative analysis has moved, in a striking way, into political science. This is in part the result of a seminar held in 1953 by the American Social Science Research Council, the report of which recommended that comparative study, "even if it falls short of providing a general theory of politics, can pave the way to the gradual and cumulative development of theory."[9] Most interesting from our point of view was its appeal to students of international politics to

> inquire what is common to the behavior of all states instead of merely describing what is unique in the conduct of states. . . .the political scientist who abstracts from international relations that aspect of behavior which involves the response of a nation in its conduct of foreign policy to a certain objective political situation involving both *external* and *internal* factors is thereby enabled to make comparisons when those factors are repeated. Indeed it is precisely in comparisons of this kind that the principles of international politics must be sought.[10]

Despite this recommendation, students of international politics have lagged behind other political scientists in their use of the comparative approach. True, many aggregate analyses have appeared, but these are not comparative in the original sense of Durkheim or Radcliffe-Brown.[11] Rosenau, making a case for a comparative approach to foreign policy analysis, points out that even books that claim to be comparative in this original sense are often not comparative at all; they merely juxtapose chapters on the same phenomenon in different countries without attempting comparative analysis.[12]

Despite the relative neglect of the comparative approach in international politics, there is nevertheless a limited, if growing literature of comparative studies of various aspects of the field. Samuel Huntington used historical case studies to investigate the connection between arms races and war. Bruce Russett examined seventeen cases in the 1935–61 period of successful and unsuccessful deterrence in order to explore the question of what makes a commitment credible. Alan Dowty has investigated the role traditionally played by guarantees in international politics and the conditions under which they are effective. He has also compared historical international systems at different periods, concluding, significantly, that the conflict behavior of states is determined not by the logic of the system but by the logic of strategic interaction. Oran Young has analyzed, systematically and comparatively on the basis of four postwar case studies, patterns of coercion in international crisis. Finally, and most notably, there is the 1974 study of George and Smoke into the working of deterrence in American foreign policy.[13] In many ways this last is the most innovative and successful comparative study produced so far and must provide a model for future research efforts. Having presented a comprehensive analysis of current deterrence theory, George and Smoke proceed to examine exhaustively theory and practice in eleven case studies taken from the 1948–62 period. This, in turn, provides a basis for the vigorous reformulation of deterrence theory. Methodological self-consciousness and a theoretical search for valid generalization is combined, unusually, with a faithfulness to the historical record. Each case study can stand by itself as an analytic account of the episode in question.

The approach I have used here, the comparative analysis of detailed historical case studies, was not an arbitrary choice but derived from (*a*) the state of theory relating to the topic and (*b*) the limited availability of relevant data. The first point has already emerged from the discussion in Chapter 1 of current theory on threat perception in international politics. Unless some theory, however rudimentary, is available to account for the occurrence of the phenomenon, specifying relevant variables and the nature of the relations between them, any straightforward statistical-correlative study is bound to be abortive. In these circumstances a case study approach can usefully perform the role suggested by Eckstein: that of suggesting insights, ideas, and questions (the *heuristic* function) and of testing the initial *plausibility* of given hypotheses.

The second reason for my choice of the comparative approach derived from the complexity of the topic. Threat perception, it rapidly became clear, is not a straightforward, irreducible unit of analysis which can be rapidly identified, isolated, and operationalized. A preliminary attempt to use content analysis to measure the frequency and intensity of threat perception was invalidated when it became clear that the occurrence of a given verbal indicator (a word or phrase suggesting, for instance, stress) simply could not be taken as sufficient evidence for an occurrence of the phenomenon. For threat perception to be identified in a plausible manner required a much more comprehensive survey of surrounding circumstances. The mere identification of the target phenomenon entailed a detailed historical reconstruction of the episode that was well on the way toward being a case history in its own right.

Part II of this study, therefore, presents six reconstructed examples of threat perception in international crisis. They are systematically compared in Part III to determine the extent to which they are characterized by common themes and patterns—and, indeed, by significant differences. This should then help us to formulate, however tentatively, a provisional explanation of the phenomenon. The case studies are the "War in Sight" crisis of 1875 (French perceptions of Germany); the Italian invasion scare of July 1889 (Italian perceptions of France); the Liman von Sanders affair of 1913 (Russian perceptions of Germany); the Prague crisis of March 1939 (British perceptions of Germany); the Polish Corridor crisis of March 1939 (Polish perceptions of Germany); and the Turkish Straits crisis of August 1946 (U.S. perceptions of the Soviet Union).

Ideally, to avoid any suspicion of biased or unrepresentative selection, one's choice of case studies should be random. This proved, unfortunately, not to be feasible. Certainly, there is no lack of examples of threat perception: on the contrary, the subject is interesting precisely because of its frequency. The problem was to find examples of threat perception sufficiently documented by accepted standards of historical research to enable one to reconstruct events in a manner adequate for the purposes of analysis and which did not leave out obvious areas of relevance to threat perception. Adequate documentation, I believe, entails more than secondary works and contemporary journalistic accounts. At a minimum, one requires primary sources in the classic sense of diplomatic history—diaries, letters, memoranda, cabinet papers, and the like. Only in this way can one even hope to approximate to an accurate description of contemporary perceptions. At one stroke this severe requirement rules out most extant examples of threat perception in international crisis. For periods in which primary diplomatic source material is available to researchers, only a limited number of the documents have been published. For most of the post–Second World War period, primary sources are not available.

Other criteria for the selection of examples further reduced the total range of feasible research options. Principally I wished to provide as wide a geographical and historical range of cases as possible within certain limits. This is in conformity with Arend Lijphart's sensible recommendation for comparative analysis, that even where the sample is a small one, maximum diversity should be aimed at to improve the chances of instituting at least some control.[14] Thus I did my best to choose case studies involving different state actors at different points in time. A number of potential candidates had to be discarded because they would have biased the whole project toward overemphasis of one or two countries best represented in existing sources.

There were two primary limits on the generality of this set of examples, the first cultural, the second temporal. The European/North American ("Western") state system provided the exclusive framework for research because of (*a*)

the linguistic and physical accessibility of documentation,
(*b*) my basic familiarity with the actors and their history, and
(*c*) most important, the theoretical need, again cited by
Lijphart (among others) to limit to manageable proportions
the number of variables involved by choosing socioculturally
comparable examples.[15] Second, the period since 1870 was focused upon because developments in the technology of warfare and communication set it apart from preceding periods;
the mere existence of the modern press and the possibility,
initially by virtue of the telegraph, of rapid communication
with areas of importance, crucially defined the nature of the
system.

One problem of presentation—primarily an aesthetic one,
but with substantive implications—is my separation of the
historical case studies from the theoretical analysis. A more
common approach is to treat the subject under discussion
within a purely conceptual framework, drawing on historical
material, where it is felt appropriate, to justify and illustrate
the arguments put forward.[16] But this approach is open to the
criticism that the evidence is fitted to some preconceived
theory rather than systematically and objectively analyzed.
For instance, the nineteenth-century evolutionists, who
played some part in discrediting comparative analysis, were
accused of "cut and paste": "The methododology was basically argument by illustration: a given bit of ethnographic
data was selected in order to 'demonstrate some aspect of a
law' of evolution."[17] If the present investigation into threat
perception is to be genuinely exploratory—and the lack of
an accepted theoretical base or set of hypotheses leaves the
researcher with little alternative—it seems desirable to present each case study as a coherent entity in which the development of the perception of threat follows its own course
within the historical context. If acceptable case studies of different examples of the topic were already in existence, then
doubtless it would be sufficient to draw upon the historical
judgment of others. Unfortunately, apart from the Steinberg
and Bialer studies, historians pay little or no attention to

threat as a dependent variable, even in the context of studies of crisis.

Other alternatives to my own preference exist. Young divides his book into chapters, each of which discusses a separate hypothesis or related set of hypotheses in the light of four case studies.[18] Even were such a comprehensive list of hypotheses available in our case, it is still doubtful whether the distracting and clumsy discontinuity entailed by this method could be accepted. Etzioni, in a study of political unification, has an introductory conceptual section, followed by four case studies of the phenomenon, each of which is analyzed separately, and finally a concluding comparative section.[19] Neither the work in general, nor the theoretical analysis in particular, fits together into a coherent whole. Thus, the presentation adopted here, which is also basically the one used so successfully by George and Smoke in their work on deterrence, commends itself above the other alternatives.

No approach can be absolutely open-ended; this would merely lead to the fruitless accumulation of data. As Radcliffe-Brown argues, "We cannot hope to pass directly from empirical observations to a knowledge of general sociological laws or principles. The attempt to proceed by this apparently easy method was what Bacon so rightly denounced as leading only to a false appearance of knowledge. The immense diversity of forms of human society must first be reduced to order by some sort of classification."[20] Sjoberg makes the point that "certain 'invariant points of reference' or 'universal categories' are required which are not merely reflections of the cultural values of a particular social system."[21]

Required for comparative research, therefore, are (*a*) accurate operational definitions of the phenomena under investigation and (*b*) a common matrix within which data can be ordered and compared. Writing as a social psychologist, Lazarus divides the process of threat perception into four analytically discrete steps: stimulus, primary appraisal, secondary appraisal, and coping process.[22] Translated to international politics these four stages could be paraphrased as (1) occurrence of event in external environment, (2) perception and definition of event by observer, (3) exploration of alternatives and choice of response, (4) implementation of response. This simple conceptual classification (derived by Lazarus from his own research and also from an exhaustive review of the theoretical and descriptive literature) is helpful as a means of operationally defining threat and identifying the salient characteristics of the phenomenon. In practice these stages are not necessarily self-contained but are likely to be chronologically overlapping. Their separation is first and foremost a conceptual one with the practical purpose of indicating to the researcher those aspects of the topic relevant to its reconstruction.

In concrete terms threat perception can be recognized by four indicators related to the above classification: (1) articulations of the decisionmakers—expressions of judgment and of personal reaction to the threatening signal; (2) descriptions by observers (foreign diplomats, officials, etc.) of the state of mind and personal reactions of decisionmakers; (3) exploration by the decisionmakers of alternative responses to the threat, with this exploration marked by intensive internal consultation, a general increase in the flow of messages into and out of the actor, a search for external support, etc.; (4) "coping processes" put into effect by the decisionmakers in response to the threat—including the strengthening or mobilization of resources (military, industrial, financial, depending on the nature of the threat), diplomatic countermoves, attack or defense, perhaps compliance. Any single one of these indicators can obviously be present without there being a threatening situation. It is the *convergence* of evidence that enables the researcher to determine whether or not there is a perception of threat—and it is the perception of decisionmakers that is of interest. By *decisionmakers* I mean those ministers and officials who participate in the conduct of foreign affairs and have unrestricted access to the relevant information. No assumptions are made about the significance of their roles in the foreign policy process, though, in practice, the nature of the documentation limits one to the main participants. What I am primarily interested in is not the process of decisionmaking in crisis as such but rather the perceptions of men with responsibility and full information.

The framework within which the case studies are presented falls into three parts which, for stylistic reasons, mesh into each other. First, there is the framework of events—the chronological unfolding of the episode—providing the backbone of the case study. Here I have clearly relied on my sense of what is or is not relevant to an understanding of the crisis. Since I am not interested merely in providing a straightforward historical account, nor do I have the space to do so, I have been obliged to maintain a concise narrative without sacrificing intelligibility. Second, there is what Knorr calls the "cognitive process of appraisal"—that is, the development and logical structure of decisionmakers' threat perceptions. Here I have tried, so far as possible, to let the record speak for itself. Finally, there are the background factors—what Singer, Pruitt, and Knorr call the "predispositions" of the observer and Lazarus calls "a constellation of ideas and expectations" to which information is assimilated. It would be impossible to list all the background factors which might be of operative significance in a given situation (nor, if we are interested in arriving at general propositions, do we have to do so[23]). The following factors, therefore, should not be considered to be exclusive but merely a working guide, based upon the studies of Singer, Pruitt, Knorr, Steinberg, and Bialer, to what might (or might not) be relevant in a particular case:

1. Previous relations between the perceiver of the threat and the source of the threat, including historical as well as recent events;
2. Any previous experience of threat on the part of the perceiver, and other personal characteristics with a bearing

on the subject, including such psychological factors as exaggerated anxiety and mistrust, personal attitudes, and philosophical beliefs;
3. The balance of capabilities between the relevant actors, which shall be defined broadly to include diplomatic capabilities, military and economic means, and the help of allies;
4. Structural factors such as the influence of bureaucratic forms and procedures, institutional interests, and contingency planning;
5. The juridical framework (including agreements, international law, and norms of behavior) within which relations between the relevant actors are conducted;
6. The policy and interest of the perceiver in the area or issue in question.

A final word is in order about the status of my research results. Given such a small sample, the high degree of personal judgment involved, the rather broad nature of the analytical categories, and the absence of a control group, any conclusions must be plausible and suggestive rather than definitive. As George and Smoke point out, since any sample using the comparative approach is neither complete nor representative, it cannot determine the relative frequency of correlations of given variables. Nor can any results be considered verified to the same degree as statistical generalizations grounded in quantitative analysis of a large number of cases.[24] Nevertheless, one must agree with Arend Lijphart that although the method can only lead to partial, and not universal, generalizations, it is still useful as a first step, to be later replicated in different settings, operationalized more rigorously for the purposes of statistical-correlative analysis, and, one hopes, improved upon or even disproved.[25] It is an essentially preliminary exploration.

Part II
Case Studies

Chapter 3

France and the
"War in Sight" Crisis of 1875

Background

   Franco-German relations after the war of 1870 were characterized, on both sides, by suspicion and hostility. Germany was convinced that France was intent on a war of revenge and cited French rearmament as proof of this.[1] Tension was maintained by Bismarck's *Kulturkampf* against the internal and external influence of the Roman Catholic Church, which found one expression in his attacks on the French clergy.[2] Thus the idea of a German preventive attack was discussed by British diplomats even before the end of the German occupation in September 1873.[3]

   In France itself there was a continual fear of renewed war with Germany. In contrast with German power, the defeat of 1870 had left France with only the remnants of an army and without allies. After 1873 restitution of the army became one of the principal preoccupations of the French government and Assembly. Especial attention was paid to the construction of fortifications around Paris and on the eastern frontier.[4]

   Meanwhile France's greatest need, as the Duke Decazes,

foreign minister from December 1873 in the monarchist government of the Duke de Broglie, saw it, was a long period of
quiet rehabilitation. Accordingly, he defined his policy as
one of "appeasement"; peace was France's "first and keenest
desire; everything which could strengthen it would be welcomed."[5]

Against a background of mistrust and fear of a second war,
the war scare of 1875 was merely one episode—albeit the
most serious—in a continuing series of alarms: In April 1872,
while German troops were still on French territory, an article
in the London *Daily Telegraph* speaking of a German ultimatum aroused disquiet.[6] In December 1873 a series of articles in the German press attacking "Ultramontane" influence
led the French ambassador in Berlin to believe, at one point,
that the possibility of a German attack was not an idle sup-
position. During 1874 Decazes was subject to spells of anxiety
about the intentions of the German government. In March
disturbing reports were received from London and Munich.
In July it appeared that the British government seriously
feared another war. Finally, in October, an ambiguous reference by the German emperor caused alarm.[7]

French perceptions in the crisis

On 5 March, 1875, after the German press had accused
France of buying horses for military purposes, an Imperial
Decree prohibited the export of horses from German territory. Decazes connected this step with a recent German demand to the Belgian government—which had pointedly been
brought to his attention—that legislation be introduced to
protect the German government against "Catholic ill-will."
Decazes believed (wrongly) that a similar move had been
made in Rome. Taken together these moves seemed to be
"symptoms" of "a complete program of political activity."
Though Belgium had rejected the German demand, would
the matter be allowed to rest there? "Foreign interference
with internal legislation" was disturbing. Decazes concluded that here was a warning of "impending trouble": Germany's "sinister schemes" were evident.[8]

German sources, including Bülow, the secretary of state for foreign affairs, continued to accuse France, despite repeated denials, of military preparations.[9] Meeting with the British ambassador on 11 March, Decazes described the current situation as "a serious and immediate peril" and expressed the hope that Britain would use her influence in the cause of peace.[10] By the following day he could write to St. Petersburg that he felt reassured and did not expect further developments. What had worried him had been the combination of the German moves in Brussels and Rome together with the prohibition on the export of horses and the tone of the official German press.[11] Again on 15 March, however, Lord Lyons found Decazes "in a greater state of alarm about the intentions of Germany than anything specific he told me seemed to warrant."[12]

Now came the main crisis. In February Radowitz, a confidential agent of Bismarck, had visited St. Petersburg. At the end of March the French representative in the Russian capital reported that the purpose of the mission had been to offer Russia a free hand in the Near East if Russia would tolerate a new war against France; the offer had been rejected.[13] (Research in the German and Austrian state archives confirms the accuracy of this report.)[14] Then on 2 April the Marquis d'Harcourt reported from Vienna that the Prussian government had placed orders with a local factory for the supply of fifty million cartridge casings and with Krupps' for four hundred cannon. Both orders were to be delivered within three months. Further information converging on Vienna from different parts of Germany confirmed that Prussia was preparing to complete her armaments by the end of June. The prohibition on horse exports was consistent with this analysis.[15] Decazes was disturbed by the news.[16]

Meanwhile the Austrian emperor and the king of Italy were meeting in Venice. Decazes saw this as evidence of their disquiet at the *Kulturkampf*. He was convinced that the Italian government, for one, believed itself "under the threat of a dangerous blow." A disturbing element had been introduced into European politics.[17] On 5 April Decazes "ex-

pressed considerable anxiety" to Lord Lyons "with regard to
the possible hostile intentions of Germany towards France."
He spoke of "an immense accumulation of munitions of war"
underway in Germany and mentioned the Radowitz mission.
Communications with Germany "were almost unnaturally
free from asperity"—the lull before the storm.[18]

The situation deteriorated still further. There appear to
have been intelligence reports predicting an almost immediate war.[19] On 5 April the *Kölnische Zeitung* published an
article accusing France of preparing a war of revenge: a
"Catholic League" of France, Italy, Austria, and the Vatican
had been formed against Germany; the recent French Cadres
Law was further proof of hostility.[20] On 9 April the Berlin *Post*
asked the question "Is war in sight?"[21]

Writing to the Marquis d'Harcourt on 9 April, Decazes
expressed mixed feelings. On the one hand he was encouraged by the Venice meeting as a sign of German isolation.
On the other hand there was the *Post* article and the cancel-
lation by the emperor Wilhelm of a planned visit to Italy:

> Here are many symptoms of discontent of which we cannot
> very well appreciate the bearing, but which we must take
> into account . . . it is said that military preparations are taking
> place in Germany; it is announced from Frankfort that army
> contractors have been ordered to make enormous provisions
> in view of possible events. From Germany, it is true, I have
> received no recriminations or exhortations. . . . But when
> Frederick the Great thought the hour had come, he invaded
> Silesia without warning Maria Theresa, and in 1792 the
> Prussian declaration of war came a fortnight after the attack.
> I conclude that, if it please Prince Bismarck to invade us, he
> will not trouble to get up a quarrel, and he will face the
> moral disapprobation of Russia and the epistolary re-
> proaches of Queen Victoria by a *fait accompli*.[22]

Any reservations were removed the following day by an
article in the official *Norddeutsche Allgemeine Zeitung*, which
singled out France from among the Catholic powers for accusation: French measures of military reorganization were

not defensive in intent but had a more definite and disquieting objective.[23] In Paris popular opinion believed a German attack was imminent; there was "great dismay" on the Stock Exchange;[24] the British representative found the French government in a "pitiable condition of terror."[25] President MacMahon and Decazes did their utmost to reassure Hohenlohe, the German ambassador, about the purpose of French rearmament.[26] Decazes privately described the German charge as "the prelude to an action of which I cannot foresee all the bearings." Bismarck would choose for France "the terrible lesson through which he intends to cure Europe of her relative independence." The Old World was to be "mastered and laid under the yoke of German terror."[27]

The panic, however, was not long at its height. In the face of various diplomatic assurances Decazes found it difficult to sustain the hypothesis of an impending German attack.[28] Nevertheless, anticipating a recurrence of the scare, he began to prepare at least two complementary courses of counteraction: first, he sounded out his ambassador in St. Petersburg (Le Flô, who had formed close links at the Russian court) as to the possibility of a Russian diplomatic intervention in Berlin, which Czar Nicholas II was to visit in May;[29] second, he approached the Paris correspondent of the *Times* of London with the idea of an *exposé* in the press which would bring the situation to the attention of Europe in general and Russia in particular.[30]

If Decazes sought a pretext to put his plan into action, this was soon provided. At a dinner on 21 April, Radowitz put forward to Gontaut-Biron, the French ambassador in Berlin, the theory of the legitimacy of preventive war: Since France was bent on revenge, why should Germany wait until she was strong? Never, Gontaut-Biron wrote Decazes, had Bismarck's "attitude been revealed to me so clearly, so neatly, or with such authority."[31] Gontaut-Biron's personal view was that certain problems of equipment and the age of the emperor made war unlikely; he wondered if the whole point was not to bring pressure on France to alter the Cadres Law.[32] Decazes accepted this analysis but told Adams, the British representative, that he was particularly worried by the Radowitz thesis, arguing that it showed "a determination on the part of Prince Bismarck to attack France, not perhaps tomorrow, but at some, probably not distant moment, which is as yet undefined and to crush her forever." France was to be permitted neither to make alliances nor to put herself into a state of defense.[33]

Decazes now launched his diplomatic counterattack. The editor of the *Times*, he learned, was ready to publish a story on German "plans."[34] On 29 April Decazes circulated his representatives throughout Europe with details of the Radowitz doctrine and instructions that its implications be raised with the respective governments.[35] Meeting with the Russian ambassador personally, Decazes painted an alarming picture of German intentions, exaggerating, as he later admitted.[36] Decazes argued that Bismarck, preoccupied with fear of a French recovery, was determined that "France must be destroyed": he was set on a preventive war that would reduce Paris within a month and two-thirds of France in a further six weeks. France's only hope rested on "words of pacification and peace" from the Russian emperor.[37]

Though there is no evidence of such a definite German invasion plan, the authenticity of Decazes's general fears is unquestionable. Just before his meeting with Orlov he had been confronted by Hohenlohe with new charges of military preparations. Decazes had denied them: war was impossible for France, and if attacked she would not fight. "Do what you like. Take Belgium, Holland, Luxemburg, it makes no difference. We shall not resist."[38] Decazes admitted to Gontaut-Biron that the "immediate and direct danger" had been removed. The real problem was "the existence beyond the Rhine of a mental attitude not only hostile to France, but fiercely opposed to its national existence."[39]

On 5 May Hohenlohe returned to Decazes and repeated that his government was not satisfied by French reassurances. At the same time Bismarck tried to minimize the area of disagreement between the two states. Decazes, still worried by the situation, understood that he was meant not to be unduly disturbed.[40] This was still not Bismarck's last word. Later that same day information was received that Bismarck had warned the Belgian king that war was imminent and that he should prepare his army to defend Belgian neutrality. Decazes's reaction was publicly restrained. He told the British chargé d'affaires: "This does not alarm me. I believe that Prince Bismarck wishes to make a successful hit (*faire un coup*); that he does not mean war, but that he wishes to frighten the King and cause the downfall of the present Belgian Ministry." Referring to the visit by Hohenlohe, Decazes gave the impression that he "felt less easy as to the position of affairs" than he did a week before.[41]

Diplomatically, events now moved to their climax. Publication in the *Times* of 6 May of a dispatch from Paris setting out German "aims" had a sensational effect. In London the French chargé d'affaires was assured that France could count on the British government.[42] Similar encouragement was received from St. Petersburg.[43] On 9 May Bismarck was delivered a tactful letter from Lord Derby, British secretary of state for foreign affairs, offering British good offices. On the tenth Gorchakov, the Russian chancellor, who had just arrived in Berlin with the czar on an official visit, requested a categorical promise from Bismarck that he would never go to war.[44]

Awaiting the outcome of his initiative, Decazes had been worried and pessimistic. In a private letter of 8 May he described his fears:

> I can see that the German Chancellor now desires to withdraw from this quarrel of his own seeking and that his design is less to make war than to profit by the terror which he inspires in order to realise a plan which has long been in his mind. He no doubt regrets having neglected to insert, amongst the clauses of the treaty which he imposed upon us, a limitation of our military forces and he no doubt intends to set as a condition to the appeasement which the Powers will demand from him their promise to impose a sort of disarmament upon us. Disarmament! As if it were possible to disarm when one has never been armed!

Decazes concluded: "I have allowed my heart to speak and you will understand this cry of despair."[45]

After his diplomatic success Decazes summarized the affair: there had been no "direct threat," but "the frame of mind revealed by the words of Radowitz and confirmed by a set of unimpeachable symptoms could only cause profound apprehension." His meeting on 5 May with the German ambassador had fitted into this pattern. Now France had won the right to reconstitute its military forces.[46] And more personally, "At last! We have escaped this terrible danger; my soul was oppressed by it; we were going to be faced with the alternative of an invasion or disarmament. . . . We knew what was meant by the *opposition* of Prince Bismarck [to others' aggressive plans] covering himself behind the exigencies of Marshall v. Moltke or the Radowitz philosophical doctrines."[47]

Chapter 4

The Italian Invasion Scare
of July 1889

Background

The scare of July 1889 was made up of three elements: Italian fears of a sudden French sea attack, of a restoration of the temporal powers of the papacy and of a Russian offensive in the Balkans. These corresponded to three of the principal areas of concern of the government of Francesco Crispi.

Crispi had long viewed France with deep suspicion. Since 1848, he believed, France had systematically opposed the movement for Italian independence; Napoleon III had done his best to maintain "a weak and disunited Italy"; and after 1870 French policy had been nothing less than "a series of acts of reprisal and malice."[1] The French annexation of Tunis in 1881 convinced Crispi that France wanted to break Italy up into a collection of republics and bid for supremacy in the Mediterranean and on the Continent.[2]

After Crispi became the Italian prime minister and foreign minister in July 1887, Franco-Italian relations rapidly deteriorated. The breakdown of tariff negotiations in February 1888 brought on a tariff war that seriously harmed the Italian economy. For the next two years friction occurred wherever the interests of the two countries touched. Throughout 1888 a series of incidents marked this state of relations.[3] The worst of these arose from the publication in September 1888 of a number of laws affecting the Italian position in the French protectorate of Tunis.[4]

Crispi's diaries of this period are full of vague suspicions of France. He accuses French agents of intriguing against Italy at various places, including Tunis, Constantinople, Abyssinia, and La Spezia.[5] In September 1887 he was worried by rumors of a Franco-Swiss agreement covering the eventuality of war between France and Italy. In December 1887 he was disturbed by French maps which seemed to indicate frontier encroachments in Tunisia.[6] He became notorious for his alarmism. Lord Salisbury, among others, described Crispi as "disturbed and alarmist" with a "liability to lumbago."[7] His biographers recognize his "tendency to suspiciousness," which he combined with belligerence, moodiness, and implacability.[8]

Just before Crispi became prime minister, the Italian government had renewed its membership, together with Germany and Austria, in the Triple Alliance. If Italy were attacked by France, Germany and Austria would be obliged to come to her assistance. At the same time the British and Italian governments had agreed in an exchange of notes to cooperate in the Mediterranean.[9] Austria and Spain later joined this agreement. Together, these accords gave Italy security on land and on sea, as Depretis, Crispi's predecessor as prime minister, told his cabinet. In line with these commitments a new naval building program, directed against France, had been launched in June 1887.[10]

Though the strength of the Triple Alliance on land was unquestioned, Crispi became preoccupied with its relative vulnerability at sea. At the end of 1887, when the technical details of military cooperation by the alliance were under discussion, Crispi had received a memorandum from Germany which pointed out that the French Fleet was "by itself as strong as the German, Austrian and Italian fleets combined." Fueling problems, moreover, would make it difficult for the German Atlantic Fleet to reach the Mediterranean. The memorandum concluded that it was of the utmost importance to obtain the cooperation of the British Fleet.[11]

Crispi and the Italian Admiralty became obsessed by fear of a French naval attack. In February 1888 a report in a London newspaper, confirmed by the German Embassy in Paris, of a concentration of French warships at Toulon, convinced Crispi that an attack was imminent.[12] In March 1888 the German military attaché in Rome reported that the Italian ministries of War and the Navy were "highly concerned that the French might appear one fine day with a fleet before La Spezia [the principal Italian naval base] and seize the harbor as a preliminary to an immediate declaration of war."[13] In the winter of 1888 Brin, the navy minister, expressed similar fears to the British ambassador. This time he talked of a French bombardment of Naples. When the Italian Fleet came to the assistance of the city, he thought, its ships would be sunk or captured. Brin went on to suggest an alliance between England and Italy but was informed that this would be unacceptable.[14] In the spring of 1889 Crispi proposed a naval convention to the Austrian government but without result.[15] As late as April 1889 Crispi was worried about lack of progress made in the strengthening of the coastal defenses at La Spezia.[16]

Rome was the second major area of concern to the Crispi government. A focus of Italian nationalist sentiment, Rome, together with the Papal States, had been under French protection until 1870, when they were incorporated in the kingdom of Italy. After 1870 the "Roman question," which arose from the refusal of the pope to recognize either the loss of his temporal power or the status of Rome as the capital of Italy, was available to France to use as a weapon against Italy. Crispi was convinced that there was widespread support in France for a restoration of the temporal powers of the pope.[17] While minister of the interior in the Depretis cabinet of 1887, Crispi had attempted to reach a settlement of the Roman question in negotiation with the clerical leaders of the conciliation movement. He had seen his efforts wrecked by French pressure on the pope.[18] The appointment of Cardinal Rampolla as papal secretary of state in the spring of 1887 confirmed the extension of French influence at the Vatican.[19]

In the Balkans Italy had a territorial claim to Trieste and the Trentino and was also interested in maintaining a balance between Austria and Russia, though Russian expansion was considered the greater danger. The second treaty of the Triple Alliance of 1887 recognized, in effect, Italian interest in the Balkans. Austria and Italy agreed to consult in the event of a change in the *status quo* and recognized the principle of compensation.[20] Crispi, personally, was eager to use Italian influence in support of Balkan nationalism.[21] Thus he strongly supported the election of Prince Ferdinand of Saxe-Coburg-Gotha to the Bulgarian throne in the face of Russian objections.[22] The Second Mediterranean Agreement of 1887—an exchange of notes between Italy, Austria, and England—expressed the common interest of these powers in preventing Russian action in Bulgaria or pressure upon Turkey which might secure for Russia a special position at the Straits.[23] In April 1889 Crispi was disturbed by reports of Russian pressure on Rumania over a question of internal security. Pointing out the danger of a Russian attack to British Prime Minister Salisbury, Bismarck, and Austro-Hungarian Foreign Minister Kalnoky, Crispi argued that "a war in the East might find an echo on the Rhine." His correspondents were not impressed.[24]

Italian perceptions in the scare

The summer of 1889 brought a renewal of Franco-Italian tension and a revival of the problem of the position of the church. On 4 June an incident at Gabes in Tunis involving the supposed ill-treatment of Italian fishermen by French officials raised afresh the unresolved question of Italian status in the protectorate.[25] Crispi made known his intention of denouncing the protocol by which Italy had suspended her capitulatory rights there.[26]

Then on 9 June, in a display of anticlerical sentiment, a statue to a sixteenth-century victim of papal intolerance was unveiled before a large crowd. Leo XIII, both insulted and afraid for his own safety, called an extraordinary and secret consistory of the cardinals at the Vatican on 30 June, at which he expressed doubts about the possibility of his continued stay in Rome.[27] He also appears to have mentioned the difficulties that would arise in the event of war between Italy and "another power." According to one source, the discussion had been purely theoretical, and no decision had been taken.[28] Crispi, however, believed throughout the crisis that the departure of the pope had been definitely agreed on and that this would be used by France as "a pretext for a quarrel with Italy which would result in war."[29] France had promised to assume the entire responsibility for the Roman question.[30]

Writing on 10 July to his minister of war, Crispi expressed anxiety about the situation:

> Europe, at the present time, is a volcano, which may burst into eruption without a moment's warning and we must be prepared. The threat of war is ever with us. The great powers are arming in feverish haste and ours is precisely the country most exposed to attack. The neighbouring Republic has made all preparations for attacking us both by sea and land. . . . No statesman can possibly wish for war and I myself even less than another, because I am aware we are not sufficiently strong, and even were we so, I should not dare to face the consequences of a conflict whose results no one can foresee.[31]

Crispi became convinced that France would attack Italy before the autumn; the king thought it "another of Crispi's exaggerations."[32]

On 12 July Crispi received a report of an imminent French attack from a "perfectly trustworthy" source.[33] (Giolitti, the minister of finance, later discovered when he became prime minister "that Crispi had this amazing information from an agent he employed at the Vatican and . . . accepted the news as true without taking the trouble to sift it.")[34] Meanwhile the official Vatican newspaper, the *Osservatore Romano*, aggravated matters by asserting "that if the Pope should be forced to exile himself from Italy he would not ask a sovereignty from any power, but would merely request a temporary hospitality, *as he would certainly return to Rome before long.*"[35] The substance of the agent's report was that at the end of October France would send her fleet into the Mediterranean in order to strike Italy a *"coup foundroyant"*. A landing in Southern Italy would be coordinated with an attack on Italy's frontiers. In the face of the numerical inferiority of the Italian Fleet and the lack of fortifications on the Italian coast, Crispi anticipated the French bombardment of towns such as Genoa, Naples, and Palermo, which "would throw the Peninsula into a panic."[36]

Crispi's immediate response to the "impending attack" was to put into effect wide-ranging defensive measures. On 13 July the king was informed of the possibility of attack and advised to form a special council consisting of himself, Crispi, the ministers of the navy and war, and the chief of the General Staff. During the following days Italy was placed on a war footing: mobilization went into effect; the fleet was placed in a state of readiness; orders were issued to complete coastal fortifications; Crispi even considered the formation of a corps of volunteers.[37]

On the diplomatic front a number of initiatives were taken. On 14 July a special envoy was sent to Bismarck to inform him of the "threatening danger,"[38] and the Italian representatives in London, Paris, Vienna, and Constantinople were recalled for consultation.[39] The chargé d'affaires in London was instructed to clarify Lord Salisbury's intentions and to request the dispatch as soon as possible of a powerful British fleet into the Mediterranean which would restrain France "from carrying her plan into execution." Crispi promised to avoid all provocation and to leave aside the Tunis question "for the moment."[40]

In addition to the French attack, Crispi began to suspect, as in April, that Russia would exploit any crisis to send a powerful army into the Balkans. Despite assurances from Kalnoky, Crispi was disquieted by a reported concentration of Russian troops on the Austrian frontier. On 20 July he learned from Reuter's agent that Russia had proposed a se-

cret agreement to Turkey, offering to guarantee Turkish territory in return for the occupation of the Dardanelles by
Russia in the event of war.[41] Meeting the British and Turkish
chargés d'affaires on 21 July, Crispi expressed "somewhat
alarming views" on the Balkan situation and appeared in a
state of "unusual excitement and general disquietude." In
his opinion there was a danger of a simultaneous outbreak of
hostilities in East and West. Crispi feared that France might
"take advantage of any disturbance in the Balkan provinces
to provoke a war with Germany and Italy." Arguing that
France was "full of illusions" about her present strength,
Crispi discounted arguments that the coming September
elections in France or the issue of a new rifle in Russia were
inconsistent with preparations for war. He "confessed to an
uneasiness which he had not felt before."[42]

In a conversation the same day with other representatives
of the diplomatic corps, Crispi poured out all his distrust and
fear of France. He saw French agents working to revive the
Irredentist movement in order to alienate Italy and Austria
"in the hope of detaching Italy from the Triple Alliance and,
in the event of war breaking out between Italy and France,
to foment the breaking out of a revolution against the Monarchical system." He referred to "the extraordinary belief of the
French in their own invincibility, even against the forces
which might be brought against them by the Triple Alliance. . . . Well accredited rumours of a large increase in the
number of troops in the south of France, notably towards the
Pyrenees, and certain naval preparations, which were reported as being hastened in the southern ports of France,
combined to create an uneasiness as to their object which he
had not before felt." His final argument was that the present
French government, afraid of an unfavorable result in the
coming elections, "might seek to unite all factions of French
opinion by making a *coup de main* against Italy."[43]

In the face of various reassurances and failing any confirmation, Crispi's fears diminished. From Berlin his special
envoy reported that the Germans were "entirely incredulous"
about his news of a French attack. Their intelligence from

Paris was that there was "no unusual massing of troops on the Italian frontier, nor any unusual activity at the arsenal in Toulon."[44] There were similar reassurances from London and Vienna.

On 1 August Crispi gave a reception to foreign heads of mission. The English chargé d'affaires inquired whether Crispi "was more satisifed with the aspect of affairs in Europe" than when he had spoken to him on 21 July. Crispi replied "that he still felt that it was impossible to predict what might happen from one week to another; but beyond vague statements as to his distrust of Russian preparations, and of a possible surprise in the East," the chargé d'affaires continued, "I could not extract any one fact upon which His Excellency's fears were based."[45]

Chapter 5

Russia and the Liman von Sanders Affair of 1913

Background

Despite the fact that Germany and Russia were members of opposing alliances, with all this entailed in terms of military planning, relations between the two countries were improving on the eve of the crisis of 1913. Sazonov, Russia's foreign minister, who had accompanied the emperor Nicholas to a meeting with the kaiser in July 1912, had received "a very favorable impression of the dispositions and intentions of the rulers of Germany." In May 1913 Nicholas had returned from a visit to Germany optimistic about the possibility of a *rapprochement*.[1] At a working level there were constructive discussions on the Armenian problem, which Russia hoped would produce a "favorable reaction on Russo-German relations in general."[2] Nevertheless, Germany could hardly be called a friendly power. In the final analysis, she would stand, as had been shown in 1909, behind Austria-Hungary in the Balkans.* The extension of German economic and political influence in the Near East, symbolized

* During the Bosnian annexation crisis of 1908–9, a virtual German ultimatum had forced Russia to back down from the side of Serbia.

45

by the Baghdad Railway scheme, had long aroused concern. Finally, anti-German feeling was endemic in Russia at the popular level.[3]

The roots of the Liman von Sanders affair lay in traditional Russian ambitions and interests at Constantinople and the Straits. As a glance at a map will show, Constantinople dominates the Straits, the sole outlet from the Black Sea into the Sea of Marmara and on to the Mediterranean. Thus, Russian policy had long been based on two principles—that no foreign power other than Turkey install itself at the Straits, and that in the long run the Straits be acquired by Russia— and it had long been accepted in St. Petersburg that ultimate measures would have to be taken to prevent the first possibility.[4] Lately it had been Germany and the Baghdad Railway scheme which aroused Russian fears of this.[5] Together with the strategic importance of the Straits (as well as the historical attachment of the Panslavs to Constantinople) were growing economic interests. In the period 1903–12, 37 percent of Russian exports went through the Straits as well as most of the grain exports by which Russia paid interest on her foreign debts.[6] "The Straits," Sazonov wrote in May 1913, "belong to Russia's incontestable sphere of interest and . . . in this respect any weakness or hesitation on our side is utterly inadmissible."[7]

These interests were threatened by the instability of the Ottoman Empire. In November 1911 an Italian threat to attack the Straits caused serious alarm in St. Petersburg. In November 1912 Sazonov was ready to send the Black Sea Fleet to the defense of Constantinople against Bulgarian attack if this proved necessary.[8] "You know how sensitive we are about Constantinople," he explained to the French ambassador.[9] The Ottoman Empire, it seemed, was on the verge of collapse. While this presented an opportunity for Russia to achieve free access to the Mediterranean at last, it also constituted a danger, for militarily, Russia was in no position to defend or advance her interests in this area.

In May 1913 the Ministry of the Marine put forward a memorandum making it clear that the weakness of the Russian Black Sea Fleet made it imperative that the Straits question be left dormant for the time being.[10] In July 1913, at a meeting to discuss the problems raised by the Turkish approach to Adrianople in the Second Balkan War, the minister of war reported that "if urgently required, an expeditionary force could be mobilized by detaching the necessary contingents from the army corps of the Odessa military district." Yet this would be of little use, as the minister of the navy admitted that "the means of transport of the Black Sea Fleet were neither sufficient nor in a good enough condition to allow a military disembarkment."[11]

In the short run at least, therefore, it was in the Russian interest to preserve Turkish integrity. As the ambassador in Constantinople, Giers, argued, Russia's advantage lay in "the establishment for the time being of sufficient order in Turkey to ensure the personal and material safety of the population, regardless of religion and nationality. This would enable us to postpone the liquidation of Turkey until the moment when our participation would afford us the greatest possible advantage."[12] But how was sufficient order to be maintained without interference from outside? To this Sazonov had no answer. In May 1913 he opposed a British proposal for European control of Turkish finances. Experience had shown, he argued, that a joint administration, financial or political, could not take the place of the sovereign power. He suspected that the proposed arrangement would "either not fulfill its purpose or lead to the hegemony of one of the Powers, for instance that of Germany."[13]

Meanwhile Sazonov was criticized in the press and in the Duma for failing to prosecute Russian interests more firmly. A foreign correspondent reported hearing criticism of Sazonov's foreign policy from all sides in July 1913. The government remained indifferent to the general dissatisfaction.[14]

Russian perceptions in the affair

The dispatch of a new Germany military mission to Turkey was first mentioned to the czar in May 1913 on his visit to Berlin. He passed on the information to Sazonov, adding that he understood it to be similar to previous German missions. Sazonov attached no particular importance to the news.[15] From May until October nothing more was heard of the mission. In October 1913 Sazonov held conversations of a "very friendly character" with Bethmann-Hollweg, the German chancellor, and Zimmermann, the under secretary of state. The von Sanders mission was not mentioned by the Germans.[16]

At the beginning of November, however, rumors of a new military mission began to be current in Constantinople.[17] On 2 November Giers reported that, in reply to his inquiry, the German ambassador had told him that there was to be a German military mission similar to the Eydoux mission of the French in Greece, which was purely instructional. Three days later, however, Giers telegraphed that the mission would not be merely instructional but that General von Sanders would also have command of the First Turkish Army Corps stationed at Constantinople.[18] Raising the question with the German chargé d'affaires, Neratov—acting foreign minister while Sazonov was at Yalta with the imperial family—pointed out that the reorganization of the Constantinople garrison under the command of a German general could not be considered "in any other way than as directed against" Russia: "Everything that transpires in Constantinople is of the highest importance for Russia." He hinted at "serious discord" if the news were not contradicted.[19] At the same time Neratov gave instructions to the Russian ambassador in Berlin to raise the issue with the German government: "Acts of this sort, causing unnecessary suspicion, hinder friendly relations with the Berlin cabinet, which are maintained on our side at such serious cost. We should not object to a command in any other part of Turkey bordering on us—but not in the capital."[20]

The German explanation, given on 10 November, was that after the Turkish failures in the Balkan Wars, their request for a new military mission could hardly be refused. It was up to the Turks where it would be based. Neratov then took the view that to station the mission in Constantinople would increase Turkey's preparedness for war in the Dardanelles region. While he did not fear the mission on the Balkan front, "Russia could not remain indifferent, if, for example, the Dardanelles were strongly fortified, and guns, which had a range of twenty kilometers over the Black Sea, were placed at its entrance. Such fortifications, constructed on the advice of German officers, could only be directed at Russia."[21]

Sazonov's personal reaction to the mission was astonishment. He could not understand why "this serious question was not touched upon by the chancellor at the time of my frank and friendly conversations with him. A German military mission in areas bordering on our frontier could not fail to provoke the violent irritation of Russian public opinion and would certainly be interpreted as an act openly hostile to us. Indeed, placing Turkish troops in Constantinople under a German general must necessarily arouse our suspicion and apprehension."[22] To Lucius, the German chargé d'affaires, he made it clear that he was "painfully disturbed" by the affair and dissatisfied by the lack of information supplied to him. The mission was "not a military but a political question of high importance for Russia."[23] Surely the mission could be stationed elsewhere, as an act of friendship? Otherwise "the Russian ambassador in Constantinople would, so to speak, be protected by a German army corps." Since Turkey had for centuries been an enemy of Russia, "it would never be agreeable to Russia that German officers should reorganize the Turkish Army." After the excellent impression made on him by his Berlin talks, the news from Constantinople had come unexpectedly. It was unfortunate that the mission had not been mentioned to him personally. When Lucius replied that it was quite out of the question for Turkey to have aggressive intentions against Russia, Sazonov retorted that "one might expect any *coup de tête* from the Young Turks." It was inadvisable to increase their "megalomania." The German officers could work, as before, in the provinces. Stationing them in Constantinople was "an entirely new thing." He concluded his remarks by saying that he staked all on friendly relations with Germany, but this turn of events made his task very difficult.[24]

Meanwhile Kokovtsov, the Russian prime minister, in Berlin on a friendly visit, was telegraphed to raise the question of the mission with the German government; the situation in Turkey, it was stressed, had been "radically altered."[25] On 18 November he discussed the problem with Bethmann-Hollweg. A military mission as such was not objected to, he said. The problem was "the German command of an army corps at Constantinople." Whether or not a military threat was involved, such a command "could not fail to raise the most serious doubts." The Straits should remain under Turkish control and Constantinople "a Turkish capital in whose integrity all the Great Powers were equally interested." A German command would place the ambassadors of the Great Powers "under the protection of Germany alone.... In the event of the slightest complications the suppression of disorder would be the responsibility of this force, and Germany would possess the task of maintaining order and security in Turkey."[26] While not fearing Turkish "megalomania," Kokovtsov thought "the matter would probably look different if Turkey should unite with other powers."[27] At a second meeting he suggested locating the command elsewhere.[28] Though he was promised nothing specific, he came away hopeful that an amicable solution could be reached and impressed by Bethmann-Hollweg's sincerity. He thought the mission had been planned in military circles.[29]

Sazonov now decided to approach the French and British governments to suggest a joint initiative at Constantinople.[30] On 25 November he discussed the situation fully with the British representative. Appearing "very seriously perturbed," Sazonov went over ground already familiar to us. One final matter, he admitted, "caused him considerable anxiety"; this was "the likelihood that the course now taken by Turkey would give rise to violent comments in the Russian newspapers which would lead to a revival of Press polemics with Germany."[31]

On 4 December Turkey announced the appointment of General Liman von Sanders as chief of the German military mission and commander of the First Army Corps in Constantinople. That very same day Sazonov had finally been promised that the question would be reexamined. News of the announcement put him in a state of "great excitement." He warned the German ambassador that "an unbearable situation" had been created for Russia. Together with France and England he would be compelled to speak to the Turks "in a very serious tone." The German garrison would make the Young Turks "intractable." There had already been indications of this. Sazonov "regretted again and again" that the German government refused to see "the eminent political significance of the question, which cannot remain without influence upon Russo-German relations."[32]

In a memorandum to the czar of the same day, 6 December, Sazonov described the strategic importance of the Straits and stated that despite this, Russia found herself incapable of mounting a serious operation in the area or even of challenging Turkish naval predominance in the Black Sea. He went on to propose that a special conference be called to study measures that could be taken to augment Russian military and naval power in the Black Sea and carefully to prepare for any action that might become necessary.[33]

At the diplomatic level Sazonov forwarded a draft note to Paris and London to be jointly presented to the Turkish government. Its text was as follows:

> The fact that the command over the Turkish Army Corps in Constantinople has been entrusted to a German general would create for him a position which hitherto neither a German nor any other officer has ever occupied in Constantinople. As a result the whole diplomatic corps would be in the power of Germany. Besides this the German general would be in a position to take military measures which might call the sovereignty of the sultan in question. The actual guarantee of the integrity of the Turkish Empire, which consists in the balance of powers, would have vanished. Indeed, if Germany should obtain such a privileged position in Constantinople, the other Powers would be forced to safeguard their interests in Turkey.[34]

In this final sentence Sazonov was not overstating his

personal view of the gravity of the situation. In a second memorandum to the czar of 5 January 1914 he requested a special conference, this time to discuss the possibility, in the event of the failure of all diplomatic efforts in the affair, of a recourse to joint military action with France and Britain. Though there was a risk of German involvement, and hence of European complications, should Russia accept the present situation it would be "a great political defeat and might have very disastrous consequences." Retreat by Russia might encourage England and France to look elsewhere for the protection of their interests.[35]

The subsequent course of the affair is beyond the scope of this chapter; suffice to say that as a result of prolonged pressure a compromise of sorts was reached. Nevertheless, irreparable damage had been inflicted on Russo-German relations—an index of the vital importance of the issue.

Chapter 6

Britain and the
Prague Crisis of March 1939

Background

The "juridical" background to the German invasion of Prague in March 1939 was provided by the Munich Agreement, which, legally binding or not, had, Chamberlain believed, established two important principles with Hitler in return for the territorial settlement. The first was contained in their mutual declaration "that the method of consultation shall be the method adopted to deal with any other questions that may concern our two countries."[1] The second was contained in Hitler's voluntary declaration that this was his "last territorial claim in Europe." Thus, now that Germany's principal and legitimate grievances against the Versailles Settlement had been conceded, Chamberlain hoped that lesser problems, such as the colonial question, could be settled more amicably. At any rate, Hitler had given his word.[2]

So far as Czechoslovakia was concerned, the British and French governments had stated their willingness at Munich to join a collective guarantee, together with Germany and Italy, of the new Czechoslovak frontiers. On 4 October 1938 the House of Commons was told that "His Majesty's Government feel under a moral obligation to Czechoslovakia to treat the guarantee as being now in force."[3] In reality the British government soon concluded that the German and Italian failure to join a collective guarantee released them from all obligation.[4] The International Commission, set up to delimit the final area of Czechoslovakia, accepted all the German demands.[5] "Arbitration" of Hungarian claims was left to Germany and Italy.[6] Lord Halifax, secretary of state for foreign affairs, wrote: "Henceforward we must count with German predominance in Central Europe." German expansion there was "a normal and natural thing."[7]

Anglo-German relations deteriorated soon after Munich. By December Chamberlain—who had been slower than Halifax and the Foreign Office to recognize German hostility—expressed his disappointment at "the continual and venomous attacks by the German press and the failure of Hitler to make the slightest gesture of friendliness."[8] In December and January there were even reports, brought before the Cabinet on 25 January, of a new German move in the west and of a planned air attack on London.[9] The return of Henderson to his post as ambassador in Berlin effectively restored Chamberlain's optimism about the prospects of peace, but Halifax remained skeptical. He wanted "more than smooth words as evidence of friendly hearts."[10] March 1939 brought with it two opposing tendencies: German efforts to lower the international temperature and fresh reports of threatening German activities, this time of an approaching German move against Czechoslovakia. Chamberlain was most impressed by the former and talked optimistically to press correspondents on 9 March, without the knowledge, and to the later disapproval, of Halifax.[11]

Munich had revealed to British policymakers one fact of central importance in this period—that Britain and France stood in a condition of "most dangerous inferiority to Germany in military strength." Britain's air defenses were seen to be seriously unprepared; Chamberlain was not alone in his horrific vision of "German bombers over London."[12] At the Anglo-French conversations of 24 November 1938 he sought

French assurance of assistance in the event of a war in which the first attack was against Britain. "London," he claimed, "was now the most vulnerable capital in the world. Within 24 hours of warfare London might be in ruins, and most of the important centres in Great Britain as well."[13] In January the Cabinet was faced with a Chiefs of Staff report that if Britain were compelled to enter a European war in the near future—for instance, in the event of a German attack upon Holland—she would "be confronted with a position more serious than the Empire had ever faced before. The ultimate outcome of the conflict might well depend upon the intervention of other powers, in particular of the United States of America."[14]

British perceptions in the crisis

By 14 March it was clear that German troops, following an appeal by the Slovak prime minister,* were about to move into Czechoslovakia. In answer to a question, Chamberlain told a "seriously disturbed" House of Commons[15] that the British guarantee was against "unprovoked aggression" and that this had not yet taken place.[16] At a policy meeting in the Foreign Office it was agreed that no "empty threats" should be made, since Britain would not fight for Czechoslovakia. The prime minister might make a statement deploring the departure from the Munich spirit, however.[17] Henderson was instructed to inform the German government on similar lines, without desiring "to interfere unnecessarily in matters with which other Governments may be more directly concerned."[18]

German troops entered Prague on the morning of 15 March. A protectorate was announced over Bohemia and Moravia; the Czechoslovak Republic ceased to exist. At 11:00 A.M. Foreign Secretary Halifax reported to the Cabinet: While "futile lectures" should be avoided, he said, public opinion should be left in no doubt as to the British attitude; a scheduled visit by Stanley, president of the board of trade, to Ger-

---

* Father Tiso was dismissed by President Hacha on 10 March. The following day he appealed to Germany for protection.

many, would be "highly undesirable." He was, however, opposed to recalling the ambassador. Personally, he strongly condemned the German action: "This was the first occasion on which Germany had applied her shock tactics to the domination of non-Germans . . . it was important to find language which would imply that Germany was now being led on a dangerous path. . . . Germany's attitude in this matter was completely inconsistent with the Munich Agreement. Germany had deliberately preferred naked force to the methods of consultation and discussion." Chamberlain, more concerned with practical details, avoided judgment. Halifax's recommendations were generally accepted: disapproval without rhetoric.[19] This was the line adopted in statements to Parliament that afternoon, except that the prime minister went beyond the prepared draft to a personal defense of Munich and an appeal for a continuation of the "search for peace."[20]

To the German ambassador, Halifax was outspoken in his condemnation. Nobody now "felt the assurances of the German Government to be worth very much." In what direction were "the next adventures" to be framed? It seemed as if Germany were seeking to "dominate Europe and, if possible, the world" by force. Hitler, however, could no longer count on "bloodless victories": "one of these days he would find himself up against something that would not be bloodless."[21]

It soon became clear that the government had failed to take account of feeling in the party. At question time in the House of Commons on 16 March the prime minister was pointedly asked by Lady Astor, who had always strongly supported him personally, whether he would lose no time in letting the German government know with what horror the whole of the country regarded Germany's action.[22] Members of both parties were "deeply disturbed" about the issue. Feeling tended to be in favor of vigorous action, such as some more comprehensive form of national service. A speech to be made by Chamberlain in Birmingham the next day was awaited with interest.[23] The crucial approach to the prime minister about this strength of feeling came from Halifax:

He now told the Prime Minister that the moment had come when Britain's attitude to further German aggression must be forcefully proclaimed, and that the Party, the House of Commons, and above all the British people demanded that this should be done with no further delay. The Prime Minister was to make a speech at Birmingham on 17 March . . . he must seize the opportunity of this much advertised occasion to make the policy of the Government plain. If he failed to do so he must expect insurrection both in the Conservative Party and the House of Commons.[24]

Into the Foreign Office, meanwhile, poured rumors and warnings of further German moves; Danzig, Memel, and Rumania were all said to be threatened.[25]

On the following day, 17 March, before setting off for Birmingham, Chamberlain again discussed the situation with Halifax. It was agreed that Henderson would be ordered home to report.[26]

Chamberlain began his speech that evening by excusing his statement of 15 March. With only partial information he had been obliged to make "a very restrained and cautious exposition." People had wrongly thought that he did not feel strongly on the subject. He then defended the Munich Agreement in detail. But "if that policy were to succeed, it was essential that no power should seek to obtain a general domination of Europe"; and Hitler had repudiated his Munich assurances, thereby raising doubts about the reliability of any further assurances he might give. Previous events might have been justifiable "on account of racial affinity or of just claims too long resisted. . . . But the events which have taken place this week in complete disregard of the principles laid down by the German Government itself seem to fall into a different category, and they must cause us all to be asking ourselves: 'is this the end of an old adventure, or is it the beginning of a new?'" In terms of policy changes, Chamberlain's recommendations were modest: consultation with France and the Dominions. He was "not prepared to engage this country by new unspecified commitments."[27] Despite his failure to suggest new policies, his position in the party was "immensely strengthened."[28]

Meanwhile, a crucial meeting had taken place in London. Tilea, the Rumanian ambassador, told Halifax that "an almost immediate thrust upon Rumania" by Germany could not be excluded. In the past few days various economic requests had been received in return for a guarantee of Rumania's frontiers. "This seemed to the Rumanian Government something very much like an ultimatum." What action would His Majesty's Government take in the event of aggression?[29] Tilea's story was confirmed by a telephone call from Elliot, the minister of health, in Paris.[30]

This meeting was a turning point in British policy. As Halifax had told American ambassador Kennedy, British policymakers had had to choose between two alternatives, the one, loosely termed "collective security," expressed in the League Covenant and Geneva Protocol, and the other involving an "avoidance of commitments . . . unless the country concerned was itself the object of attack." One's choice "depended very greatly upon the estimate . . . formed upon the possibilities or otherwise of his own country being the object of direct attack." Halifax "had little doubt that recent events would have the result of leading many people to examine afresh . . . general cooperation."[31] That very evening inquiries were sent out concerning the position of the Soviet, Greek, Polish, Yugoslav, and Turkish governments in the event of German aggression against Rumania.[32]

The crisis was now at its height. Despite a denial from the Rumanian foreign minister that his government had received an "ultimatum" from Germany, Tilea himself declined to withdraw his story, and there was further confirmation of it from French sources.[33] Information continued to arrive of imminent German moves against Memel and Danzig.[34] At a Cabinet meeting on the afternoon of 18 March Chamberlain explained that he regarded his Birmingham speech as a challenge. "It followed that if Germany took another step in the direction of dominating Europe, she would be accepting the challenge." Thus Rumania was of more than strategic importance but "raised the whole question whether Germany intended to obtain domination over the whole of South Eastern Europe."[35] The government's next step was to find out who would join Britain in resisting aggression.[36]

The issue was more than that of Czechoslovakia or even Rumania. Halifax telegraphed on 20 March: "In spite of doubts as to accuracy of reports of German ultimatum to Rumania, recent German absorption of Czecho-Slovakia shows clearly that German Government are resolved to go beyond their hitherto avowed aim of consolidation of German race. They have now extended their conquest to another nation and if this should prove to be part of a definite policy of domination there is no State in Europe which is not directly or ultimately threatened."[37]

Chapter 7

Poland and the Corridor Crisis of March 1939

Background

Polish-German relations in the second half of the 1930s were based on two premises, one juridical, one intellectual. The former was the German-Polish Declaration of 26 January 1934, which affirmed that the two governments would "settle directly all questions whatsoever which concern mutual relations." If this proved impossible, other peaceful means would be employed, and the use of force was ruled out.[1] One index of the functional relevance of this declaration is the extent to which Beck, Poland's foreign minister from 1932 to 1939, referred to it.[2] The intellectual premise (on the Polish side) underlying German-Polish relations was the assumption that fundamental antagonism between Nazi Germany and Soviet Russia made Poland an indispensable partner of Germany.[3] This fundamental antagonism, moreover, enabled Beck to pursue the policy of balance between his two great neighbors which he believed to be a historical condition of Polish independence.[4]

Until the *Anschluss* and Munich, Hitler undoubtedly needed to maintain Polish good will, and although there were local incidents at Danzig, the Poles were assured that the German government had no intention of altering the statute of the Free City.* On 24 October 1938, however, Germany proposed a "general settlement" of issues between Poland and Germany, including the return of Danzig to the Reich and the building of an extraterritorial motor road and railway line across Pomerania. In return, Poland would be assured railway and economic facilities in Danzig, a twenty-five-year extension of the 1934 agreement, and a guarantee of the Polish-German frontier.[5] Beck rejected these proposals out of hand. Stressing the vital nature of Poland's attachment to Danzig, he could only suggest replacing the existing League guarantee by a Polish-German agreement guaranteeing existing rights: "Any tendency to incorporate the Free City in the Reich," he warned, "must inevitably lead to a conflict not only of a local character, but also jeopardising Polish-German relations in their entirety."[6] Despite the shock of these proposals, Beck "did not believe that this attitude marked a change in the policy of Hitler and the Third Reich" towards Poland.[7] But in January 1939 the proposals were repeated, this time by Hitler in a conversation with Beck in person. Hitler declared: "Danzig is German, will always remain German, and will sooner or later become part of Germany."[8] Beck, hearing "quite new accents" in Hitler's speech, returned to Warsaw with the warning "that the situation on the Danzig problem was becoming serious."[9] As in November 1938, Beck's confidence was quickly restored. A visit by Ribbentrop to Warsaw at the end of January and a speech to the Reichstag on 30 January in which Hitler mentioned Poland "in sympathetic terms" convinced Beck that German-Polish relations were basically unchanged.[10] He told Rumanian Foreign Minister Gafencu that he was sure the Danzig problem could be "settled amicably."[11] In general he discounted the

* According to the Treaty of Versailles of 1919, Danzig, a Baltic port with an overwhelmingly German population, became a free city in treaty relations with Poland and part of the Polish customs area, with the conduct of its foreign relations entrusted to Poland. Hitler made his assurance in November 1937.

possibility that Hitler had immediate ambitions in the east; he believed Hitler's attention was concentrated on the west and on colonies.[12]

The importance which Beck imputed to Danzig can be accounted for in a number of ways. At one level Danzig was a principal component in Beck's conception of Poland as a Baltic state.[13] The port was also of considerable maritime and commercial significance, situated as it was at the mouth of the Vistula, Poland's largest river. Historically, there was the emotive point that the partition of Poland at the time of Frederick the Great had begun with the separation of Danzig from the Polish hinterland. Finally, the Poles had been taught by Pilsudski that the Danzig question constituted a criterion for evaluating Germany's relations with Poland.[14]

Polish attitudes toward Czechoslovakia, the other area of importance in the March crisis, were rather different. Beck had long felt that the destruction of Czechoslovakia was in the Polish interest. It would enable Polish annexation of the Teschen-Silesia area, which, though it had a large Polish population, had gone to Czechoslovakia in 1919. It would also, Beck hoped, weaken Soviet influence in Central Europe. Most important, it would allow the emergence of an independent Slovakia, amenable to Polish influence and blocking Germany in the south, and, through the incorporation of Subcarpathian Ruthenia by Hungary, secure a common Polish-Hungarian frontier, desired in the creation of a "Third Europe" of smaller powers, independent of the great powers to east and west.[15] Not only was the disintegration of Czechoslovakia desired; it was even discussed in the Polish Foreign Office after Munich as an imminent possibility.[16]

Polish perceptions in the crisis

From the early stages of the internal crisis in Czechoslovakia, Polish attention was focused on the fate of Slovakia. The view was expressed by Polish officials that a union of Slovakia with either Bohemia or Hungary, or "a truly independent Slovakia," would be regarded "with benevolence." "What Poland would dislike would be a Slovakia nominally

independent but in fact dominated by Germany."[17] On 14
March Father Tiso, the Slovak prime minister, returned from
Germany to declare the independence of Slovakia. Events
had developed, one Polish official complained, "very quickly
and without any consultation between Warsaw and Berlin."[18]
Indeed, the Poles had been trying unsuccessfully since 11
March to make contact with the German government.[19]

By the morning of 15 March Prague had been occupied
by German troops, and Father Tiso officially requested that
Slovakia be placed under German protection. A protectorate
was announced the following day. Further east, Subcarpathian Ruthenia was annexed by Hungary.

In Warsaw, Slovak "independence" was recognized immediately on 15 March. Polish officials admitted to Kennard,
however, "that the Polish Government had been surprised at
the rapidity of the developments of the last two days. They
had expected that the Czechoslovak Government would
largely become subservient to the Reich, but they had not
thought that Germany would absorb Bohemia and dominate
Slovakia with such rapidity." The achievement of a common
frontier with Hungary provided small encouragement: it
"would form no barrier to Germany's further penetration
eastward."[20] In Danzig there was talk of "an early radical
change in the status of the Free City," to be answered by
Poland with "armed resistance."[21] The extension of German
protectorates over most of the former area of Czechoslovakia
seems to have produced "consternation" in military circles.[22]
Poland's weakened strategic position was apparent to any observer: its western defenses were completely outflanked and
new avenues of invasion opened up.[23] Contacts were reported
to have begun between the Polish and Hungarian general
staffs to establish closer military cooperation.[24]

The reaction of the Foreign Ministry was one of concern.
On the evening of 16 March the German ambassador was
asked for "a genuine interpretation of the Tiso-Hitler declaration" of a protectorate over Slovakia. Lipski, the Polish ambassador in Berlin, was telephoned instructions for a
conversation with Göring on the seventeenth. The very fact,

he was to say, that Poland was faced with "ever new decisions without previous notification" did "not contribute to the creation of a good atmosphere in Polish-German relations." Nevertheless, Lipski did take away from his meeting with Göring the impression of "a desire to maintain good relations."[25] Other diplomatic consultations took place with the Hungarian, Rumanian, Lithuanian, Latvian, and Estonian governments.[26]

While some observers were reporting "consternation in Poland" and the unofficial Polish press was writing of a Poland face to face with its destiny,[27] Beck adopted a far calmer tone. He denied to the British ambassador the danger of a German move against either Danzig or Memel and expressed the hope "that a protectorate might not be established over Slovakia to the same degree as over Bohemia and Moravia."[28] When Kennard returned the next day with news of a supposed German "ultimatum" to Rumania, Beck reacted incredulously: "He had quite recently received assurances in Berlin that the Reich regarded Hungary's claim on Rumania as unjustifiable and that they would give them no encouragement . . . he could not believe, although everything was possible these days, that the German Government would at this moment present what amounted to an ultimatum to the Rumanian Government."[29]

Meanwhile the press was printing such statements as "What we won with our blood we will defend with our blood." In Warsaw there were demonstrations against Beck and his "pro-German policy." On 19 March the president broadcast an appeal for sacrifice. On 20 March Lipski returned from Berlin bent on resignation, hoping "to bring the country back to its senses." He reported the French view that Hitler's next blow would be directed east, against Rumania and Poland. This upset Beck.[30] He continued, however, to discount the possibility of a move against Danzig. What worried him just at this moment was the tense state of relations between Hungary and Rumania. His deputy minister, Arciszewski, took the view that there might be collusion between Germany and Hungary but did not believe that Poland was included in German designs, "at all events in the near future." He thought that "a Russian or Ukraine adventure was more probable."[31]

On 21 March Lipski, now back in Berlin, met with Foreign Minister Ribbentrop. The meeting proved critical. Lipski complained that there had been no understanding over the Czech question, which was bad enough, since the Czechs "were after all a Slav people. But in regard to Slovakia the position was far worse." He emphasized both Polish cultural affinity with Slovakia and their long common frontier. The German protectorate, therefore, was "directed against Poland." It was "a serious blow" to German-Polish relations. Ribbentrop, in turn, suggested that Lipski return to Warsaw to discuss German proposals over Danzig, which he repeated. "He advised that the talk should not be delayed, lest the Chancellor come to the conclusion that Poland was rejecting all his offers."[32]

The following day, Lithuania ceded Memel to Germany.* Lipski returned to Warsaw from Berlin in an "extremely pessimistic" frame of mind. He thought that while Ribbentrop had preserved the formalities of politeness, "basically his remarks were violent; for instance, he declared that Germany had contributed to the establishment of Poland." Lipski "did not exclude Germany's formulating its demands in the form of an ultimatum." Poland was being encircled. Lubienski, Beck's chef de cabinet, agreed: the conversation was "very disturbing," and "he did not rule out the possibility of a German ultimatum over Danzig." At any rate, a German guarantee was worthless, and any concession would only lead to further demands. Beck, personally, was caught in a dilemma. On the one hand his foreign policy was under "very serious

---

* Memel was a Lithuanian port on the Baltic with a predominantly German population, which had been forcibly seized by Lithuania in 1923. Ribbentrop had made no mention of the impending cession of Memel in his conversation with Lipski on 21 March. In his instructions to Lipski of 25 March, Beck complained that the Polish government had not been informed of the German moves against Slovakia and Lithuania, "although they concerned territories right on the frontiers of the Polish Republic."

criticism." On the other he was worried that some gesture, such as the British idea of a Four Power Declaration (see, Chapter 6, note 37), "might provoke an immediate attack by Germany."[33] Moreover, he had no wish to draw the Soviet Union into European affairs.[34] The solution which he now suggested was a secret agreement of consultation between Britain and Poland. Poland would not follow Czechoslovakia and Lithuania over Danzig, he told Kennard; he would not submit to dictated terms.[35] Meanwhile, the Polish command, counting on a possible synchronization of the cession of Memel with an attack on Danzig, took steps for military cover of the city.[36]

On 23 March there were further ominous developments. First, the terms of the German-Slovak Agreement were issued. Germany was to have control over the armed forces and military policy of Slovakia and the right to maintain such military establishments and forces as it considered necessary. The construction of strategic works had already commenced.[37] Second, an announcement was made of a trade agreement between Germany and Rumania which provided Germany with far-reaching rights in the exploitation of Rumanian minerals and oil and virtual control over the economic life of the country.[38] That day Smigly-Rydz, commander of the Polish armed forces, issued special instructions defining the war tasks of the western armies. A partial mobilization was ordered, and four divisions were moved up to the East Prussian frontier. Thirteen trains of rolling stock were withdrawn from Danzig.[39] In Warsaw a three-day air-raid exercise and blackout were ordered.[40]

At the Foreign Ministry Beck addressed a conference of senior officials. The situation, he admitted, was "tense" and "serious." Germany, one of the two factors which had always determined Poland's position, had "lost its sense of responsibility," which it had always kept until then, even in difficult circumstances. Because of this "a series of new elements" had appeared in Polish politics and "a series of new problems" faced the state. The limits beyond which Polish policy would not go had been defined and included an infringement of Polish territory and the unacceptability of an imposed solution in Danzig. Danzig, besides its objective importance, was a symbol. If the Poles allowed themselves to be dictated to, there was no knowing where it would end. The "enemy" was a troublesome element, since he seemed "in effect to have lost all proportion in his thought and action." Opposed by a determined attitude, he might regain this. Germany was marching across Europe with nine divisions but would not overcome Poland with such forces; Hitler knew this.[41] He concluded: "We have arrived at this difficult moment with all the trump cards in our hand. This does not speak badly for us."[42]

Chapter 8

The United States
and the Straits Question, 1946

Background

The year 1946 saw progressive deterioration in Soviet-American relations. Confrontation at the United Nations over the Soviet failure to withdraw from Northern Iran; Soviet assistance to Communist, antigovernment forces in China, Korea, and Greece; the breakdown of economic cooperation in a divided Germany; sterile invective at the Conference of Foreign Ministers in Paris—all went to create that situation which became known as the Cold War.

A Soviet-American conflict of interests in the Near East, of which the Straits question was but one aspect, was a particularly significant factor in this mutual dynamic of suspicion and hostility. As early as January 1946 President Truman had become convinced that the Soviet Union intended an invasion of Turkey and a seizure of the Straits.[1] Kennan, in his deeply influential memorandum of February 1946, predicted Soviet efforts to advance the official limits of its power and gave Northern Iran and Turkey as examples of such areas of pressure.[2] Simultaneously, the Joint Chiefs of Staff were forcefully arguing that, from the military standpoint, the consolidation and development of Soviet power now constituted "the greatest threat to the United States in the foreseeable future." Iran was given as the latest example of Soviet expansion.[3] On 5 March the Soviet government was informed in an official note that the United States could "not remain indifferent" to the continued presence of Soviet troops in Iran.[4]

Iran, indeed, almost became the occasion for the first crisis of the Cold War. On 6 March movements of Soviet troops and equipment southward to Teheran and possibly towards the Turkish and Iraqi frontiers were reported. Secretary of State Byrnes believed an invasion of Iran to be imminent and remarked to his aides "that it now seemed clear that the U.S.S.R. was adding military invasion to political subversion" in that country. Beating one fist into the other hand he dismissed them with the comment: "Now we'll give it to them with both barrels."[5] Truman actually mentioned the possibility of a war with the Soviet Union over Iran.[6]

The United States' interests in the Near East were first of all a function of its commitment, which cannot be overstressed, to the United Nations and the principles which the organization embodied. Any disagreement between the Soviet Union and Turkey or Iran was a test of the United Nations. A failure to prevent conflict or intimidation would discredit the organization at its very outset.[7] In particular, the United States had a basic interest in the preservation of the freedom of commercial passage through the Straits. Faced with initial Soviet demands in 1945 for a revision of the 1936 Montreux Convention governing the status of the Straits,* the American position had been defined as opposition to "any proposals granting a nation other than Turkey bases or other rights for indirect military control of the Straits." If possible, the Straits were to be demilitarized.[8] Truman favored

---

* The signatories of the Montreux Convention were the USSR, Great Britain, Turkey, France, Japan, Bulgaria, Greece, Rumania, and Yugoslavia. It had placed the Straits under Turkish military occupation.

an inclusive scheme for the internationalization of the world's free waterways, including the Straits.[9]

While there was no specific United States commitment to Turkey, growing Soviet pressure over the Straits issue and territorial claims in the Kars-Ardahan region provoked increasing American interest and involvement. In February, 1946, for instance, an agreement was reached for the United States to grant Turkey a credit of $10 million to purchase war-surplus material in the Middle East, and the concept of "support of Turkey" had already been discussed.[10] As a result of the March scare the Joint Chiefs of Staff were specifically asked by the secretary of state how U.S. and U.K. security interests would be affected by Turkish concession of Soviet demands. In a crucial document the Joint Chiefs described Soviet claims as "a manifestation of Soviet desire to dominate the Middle East and the eastern Mediterranean." Since the USSR was already capable of closing the Straits whenever it wished, its quest for bases could not be justified on purely defensive grounds. Consequently, current claims could be only a prelude to further territorial demands in the Aegean area. And should the USSR ever come to dominate Turkey and the Aegean, thereby threatening the Suez-Alleppo-Basra triangle, Great Britain would ultimately have to fight or accept the eventual disintegration of its empire. If the empire dissolved, the military potential of the United States and its allies "might be insufficient to match those of an expanded Soviet Union." Clearly, then, the United States should buttress the British Empire against what the Joint Chiefs saw as aggressive Soviet imperialism.[11] In April the considered dispatch of the battleship *Missouri* to Turkey was one sign of the emergence of an expanding and autonomous American interest in the Eastern Mediterranean.[12]

The actual issue of the future of the Straits was first discussed formally by the Allies at the Potsdam Conference in July 1945. Stalin wished to terminate the Montreux Convention and to obtain military bases at the Straits. Truman opposed this. In the final protocol of the conference it was agreed that the Montreux Convention should be revised and that the United States, Great Britain, and the Soviet Union would separately communicate their views on the subject to the Turkish government.[13] Though no specific provision was laid down for resolving disagreement, the Montreux Convention itself, under article 29, called for a special conference of signatories if such a situation arose.

With respect to the balance of Soviet-American capabilities in the Near East in 1946, the inferiority of the United States was readily apparent. In an assessment of a hypothetical outbreak of hostilities with the Soviet Union submitted on 11 April 1946, the Joint Chiefs of Staff were forced to conclude that during the opening phases "the initiative would be almost completely in the hands of the enemy" and that affairs would be "almost universally unfavorable to us militarily."[14] Rapid demobilization in all branches of the armed service had left the United States in a position where it was even unable to support diplomatic initiatives, such as the Iran note of 5 March 1946, by a convincing show of force.[15]

In purely numerical terms the USSR was estimated in the summer of 1946 to have 190,000 troops in the Caucasus along the Turkish and Iranian borders, as well as 300,000 in Rumania and 90,000 in Bulgaria. Altogether, the Soviet Union had an air force of 20,000 combat aircraft, of which 3,000 were in Rumania alone. In contrast, the United States had about 350,000 men in Europe, mostly in Germany, Italy, and Austria.[16] Britain, bound to Turkey by the Mutual Assistance Treaty of 1936, had troops in Greece and 100,000 men in Egypt. In terms of its extensive obligations, however, Britain's forces were "totally inadequate."[17] Turkey was not in a position to defend itself.[18] The atomic bomb, the one decisive advantage possessed by the United States, was not a relevant factor in some distant disagreement such as those over Iran or the Straits. Furthermore, American public opinion was far from ready to acknowledge the breakdown of wartime partnership between the United States and the Soviet Union. As the American ambassador in Moscow commented, the Soviet

Union knew that the American system of government would not permit the United States to use its "temporary ascendancy in atomic power as a means of pressure."[19]

American perceptions in the crisis

On 7 August 1946 the United States government was presented with the text of a Soviet note to Turkey. Accusing Turkey of having failed to prevent the enemy in the past war from using the Straits for military purposes, the Soviet Union rejected the Montreux Convention as inadequate to present conditions and proposed the establishment of a new regime for the Straits based on five principles. The first three, relating to the passage of merchant ships and warships, were basically in conformity with the American position. The final two were not. It was proposed that

> 4) The establishment of a regime of the Straits, as the sole sea passage, leading from the Black Sea and to the Black Sea, should come under the competence of Turkey and other Black Sea Powers.
>
> 5) Turkey and the Soviet Union, as the powers most interested and capable of guaranteeing freedom to commercial navigation and security in the Straits, shall organize joint means of defense of the Straits for the prevention of the utilization of the Straits by other countries for aims hostile to the Black Sea powers.[20]

Consideration of this initiative was placed in the hands of the three departments primarily concerned, State, War, and Navy. At an early meeting attended by the secretaries of the three departments, the Joint Chiefs of Staff, and Mediterranean and Middle East experts, Dean Acheson, acting secretary of state while Byrnes was in Paris at the peace conference, described his first impressions: A grave matter has arisen affecting the foreign policy and future defense of the United States. All the services should therefore jointly canvass their policies and capabilities and recommend to the president a coordinated view and program. It was clear to Acheson that the Russians were trying to take over the Straits and establish a naval and air beachhead there, which would inevitably lead, according to the plain pattern of Russian behavior, to Turkey's loss of sovereignty. The question was simple. Could and would the United States stand by the Turks? If it decided it could and would, regardless of the consequences, then it could afford to reply to the Soviet note gently but firmly. But it must be prepared to follow its reply up.[21]

There could be little doubt about the line to be taken by the Joint Chiefs of Staff. As recently as 27 July they had submitted a comprehensive study of Soviet-American relations to the president in which they had argued that the USSR sought world domination and was employing "every means short of war" to bring satellites to heel, to acquire control of strategic areas, and ultimately to isolate the capitalist powers. Peaceful coexistence was impossible in the long run. The United States had to contain the spread of Soviet influence, basing its strategy on the assumption that only force could deter this policy of aggression.[22]

Within the State Department itself the reaction to the Soviet note was by no means unanimous. One view noted merely that the proposal conflicted with the defined position of the United States and "would cause grave concern in the War and Navy Departments." Any action that might "increase the tension between the Soviet Union and the Western powers *in a confusing side arena*" was opposed.[23] At the same time the Moscow embassy, in response to a departmental inquiry, discounted the probability of an attack on Turkey, though the "possibility" existed; indeed, Stalin had personally gone out of his way to assure a foreign diplomat that the USSR "had no intention of attacking Turkey."[24]

In contrast, Wilson, the American ambassador in Ankara, took the sternest view of Soviet aims.[25] The Soviet proposal, he argued, was not aimed at a revision of the Montreux Convention, as was agreed at Potsdam, but would establish a "new regime on a fundamentally different basis." Defense of the Straits would be solely the responsibility of Turkey and Russia, excluding other powers and the United Nations. Acceptance of such a proposal would mean the end of Turkish independence. Again, although the Soviet Union was a signatory of the Montreux Convention, its note of 7 August made no pretense of following established procedure for proposing any revision. The Soviet Union, Wilson concluded, was not really interested in any revision on its merits but merely sought to exploit the issue to destroy Turkish independence, establish a 'friendly' regime in Turkey, and thereby close the one remaining gap in the chain of Soviet satellites which extended from the Baltic to the Black Sea. To prevent this was a vital interest of the United States. If Turkey fell under Soviet control, the last barrier in the way of a Soviet advance to Suez and the Persian Gulf would have been removed.[26]

The memorandum agreed upon and presented to the president on 15 August by Acheson, secretary of the navy Forrestal, and Royall, the under secretary of state for war, developed Wilson's case and incorporated the tough line taken in the Joint Chiefs of Staff paper of 27 July. The primary objective of the Soviet Union, it was argued, was to obtain control of Turkey. This was the real purpose of introducing armed forces into the country. Once this happened it would be extremely difficult, if not impossible, to prevent the Soviet Union from extending its domination over Greece and the whole Near and Middle East. American and other interests would be gradually eliminated from the entire area. Once the USSR had obtained full mastery of this region—strategically important from the point of view of resources (including oil) and communications—it would be in a much stronger position to obtain its objectives in India and China. It was therefore in the vital interests of the United States that the Soviet Union should not succeed, by force or threat of force, in implementing its demands. Despite Turkish insistence that an attack would be resisted, it was doubtful that this determination could be maintained without an assurance of support from the United States. Moreover, it was always difficult to persuade the Russians to withdraw from a position to which they were formally committed. The only effective deterrent would be their conviction that the United States was prepared, if necessary, to meet aggression with force of arms. The time had come when the United States had to decide to resist, with all the means at its disposal, any Soviet aggression and, in particular, any Soviet aggression against Turkey.[27]

Acheson pointed out to Truman that if the Soviet Union did not back down and if the United States maintained its opposition, this might lead to armed conflict. The president replied that he had no doubt they "should take a firm position both in this instance and in China." They "might as well find out whether the Russians were bent on world conquest now as in five or 10 years." Approving the policy recommended in the memorandum, he affirmed his determination to pursue it "to the end."[28] As a first step it was decided to reply at once to a Turkish inquiry as to the position of the United States. As a sign of earnest, the newly commissioned aircraft carrier *Franklin D. Roosevelt* would be sent to join the *Missouri*, already at Istanbul.[29]

In its reply to the Soviet Union the United States explained its objections to proposals 4 and 5 of the Soviet note. Proposal 4 did not appear to envisage a revision of the Montreux Convention but rather the establishment of a new regime that would be confined to Turkey and the other Black Sea powers. The United States could not agree to the exclusion of other powers. Nor could it agree to proposal 5, that Turkey and the Soviet Union should organize joint means of defense of the Straits: "It is the firm opinion of this Government that Turkey should continue to be primarily responsible for the defense of the Straits. Should the Straits become the object of attack or threat of attack by an aggressor the resulting situation would constitute a threat to international security and would clearly be a matter for action on the part of the Security Council of the United Nations." The U.S. reply observed that the Soviet note contained no mention of the UN. The U.S. view was that the Straits regime should be consistent with the principles and aims of the UN.[30]

The reply of the Turkish government itself to the Soviet

note was, as had been recommended, both reasonable and firm.[31] After refuting at length charges of violations of the Montreux Convention, Turkey went on to deny the acceptability of the Soviet proposals. In a further exchange of notes in September neither side altered its original position. Though the Soviet note of 7 August did not lead to any alteration of the Straits regime, it did have a far-reaching effect on U.S. policy in the Mediterranean. There had been a decision to maintain Turkish independence in the face of a perceived Soviet threat to expand southward. In the words of a State Department memorandum of 21 October, it was now "the policy of the United States to give positive support to Turkey." This extended to diplomatic and economic assistance and, if necessary, military aid furnished through Britain.[32]

Part III
Analysis

Chapter 9

Clearing the Ground

At the outset of this project I defined my task as being that of investigating the conditions under which threat is perceived and explaining the occurrence of the phenomenon. In order to do this, I had first to identify the phenomenon. This may not be so easy as it sounds, for to be able to identify a phenomenon one must be able to describe it; yet until the phenomenon is actually investigated, no such description may be available or existing descriptions may be misleading. Rigid adherence to existing formulations could lead to the repetition of incorrect assumptions. In order to avoid this problem, and also epistemological objections to the possibility of knowing "mental events,"[1] I set forth a preliminary operational definition in terms of the behavioral reactions of the observer (Chapter 2). A perception of threat, in short, was defined in terms of those traits we recognize it by. Left open for empirical investigation was exactly what takes place between the occurrence of an event in the external environment and those linguistic, emotional, and political reactions of the observer which enable us to recognize that a threat has been perceived.

Perception can be defined as "sensory experience which has gained meaning or significance." It is distinguished from *sensation*, which refers to the exposure of the observer to unrefined experience—what Dewey calls "blooming, buzzing confusion." While sensation is indiscriminate and disordered, perception orders and discriminates: it filters out meaningful patterns from the confusion; it recognizes that these patterns of sense-data can be subsumed under particular and known concepts. In the psychology literature perception is argued to be inseparable from learning: "When, as the result of learning experiences, one understands the relationships of objects which were previously merely raw, undifferentiated sensory experiences, he is said to perceive these objects. The non-sensory learning experience which is essential to transforming meaningless sensory experiences into perceptions involves the development of concepts or ideas about the sensory experiences."[2] Thus perception presupposes concept learning and concept recognition. Were we not equipped by learning with those concepts relevant to the world in which we live, it is hard to see how perception would be possible at all. Equally, were, let us say, a man from Mars to land on Earth, he would doubtless perceive objects relevant to his life on Mars but would be quite incapable of perceiving—that is, of recognizing—the myriad objects and experiences irrelevant to that previous environment.

In its general usage *perception* refers to a more or less instantaneous assimilation of experience, and not to a protracted search for understanding or to an attempt at recognition. Unless the conditions of perception are especially unfavorable (a thick fog, for instance) or the object to be perceived is in a defective condition, recognition is immediate. Should perception entail a protracted attempt at reasoning or remembering rather than a more or less immediate act of recognition, we should probably be inclined to drop the description "perception." Otherwise the word, by losing its precision, would cease to be useful.

This consideration brings us back to our initial concern, that is, of providing a description of threat perception in international relations. The great temptation here is to assume that since we use the term *threat perception* (partly for want of a better one), we are therefore referring, as with *perception* as such, to a more or less immediate act of recognition. According to this version, threat would be perceived in the sense that a book is perceived. The concept of "threat" would be learned, as other concepts, such as books and tables, are learned, and a perception of threat would involve the recognition that a certain pattern of sense-data is subsumed under the concept of threat. The case for this interpretation has been made by Justin Gosling, who argues, from a philosophical perspective, that "a case of fear must be a case of some person or animal noticing something which has been learnt to be a source of hurt or harm (or which is a sign of such a source)."[3] In other words, we perceive certain phenomena to be threatening because we have learned in the past that those phenomena or one of the elements in a constellation of phenomena tend to presage the infliction of pain. The lesson may have been learned personally: once bitten, twice shy. Having been scalded by a boiling kettle, we are very likely to treat boiling kettles with extreme caution in the future. The victim of a traffic accident may find that his unease about a possible future accident precludes his driving at all. Studies in the behavior of communities struck by natural disaster do indeed demonstrate the subsequent appearance of an extreme sensitivity to the possibility of a recurrence of that disaster. We may also learn that certain phenomena are potentially dangerous from the unfortunate experience of others or on the basis of the received wisdom of the community. Thus, we take care crossing the road although the danger from traffic is something we usually learn about at second hand.

Robert Jervis has explicitly transferred this proposition from the field of personal psychology to the psychology of decisionmaking groups: "The more familiar a phenomenon is, the more quickly it will be recognized." Thus, "if a state has frequently attacked its neighbors they will quickly take ambiguous evidence as indicating renewed aggressiveness even though they know that other explanations are possible."[4]

On the basis of the case studies in Part II, this preceding account can be seen at best to be only a partial and oversimplified description of threat perception in international politics. Historical memory or learning does play a role in the process but not in the straightforward sense of perception as an act of recognition that a given set of sense-data falls under a certain linguistic description. In none of our cases could the perception of threat be equated with the recognition of a learned stimulus, as a simple list of the relevant signals demonstrates:

1875—an article in a German newspaper
1889—a report that the pope was to leave Rome
1913—the dispatch of a German military mission to Constantinople
1939—the entry of the Germany Army into Prague
      —German proposals for negotiations over Danzig
1946—Soviet proposals for renegotiation of the Montreux Convention.

In none of these cases could the perception of threat have involved the recognition of something "learnt to be a source of hurt or harm" for the reason that each of these events was quite unique. None of these signals had, in the past, presaged the infliction of harm on the observer.

Confirmation of this point is provided by an unexpected, if negative, finding of my research: the failure, almost without exception, of the decisionmakers examined to make any explicit reference to the apparently most striking lesson from their own experience, or to make any comparison between that lesson and the threatening situation immediately facing them. Were the Gosling theory of threat recognition true, one would certainly expect at least a passing mention, and probably more than that, to previous experiences of danger which had provided material for concept learning.

In the 1875 crisis there seems to be an almost systematic avoidance of any open mention of the catastrophe of 1870. In 1913 no reference can be found either to the recent Bosnia crisis of 1908–9 or to other not-uncommon examples of Russo-German abrasion. In March 1939 one finds a similar avoidance on the part of both British and Polish decisionmakers of a comparison between contemporary events and recent experiences of Germany, though these included such unforgettable episodes as the 1914–18 war! Finally, in 1946 American observers scrupulously shunned seeking any parallel between Soviet behavior and the prewar policy of Nazi Germany.[5] Each of these analogies would surely have sprung readily to mind at the time. In any event, such analogies may have come to mind, and it is inconceivable that their unconscious influence was insignificant, but pen and tongue avoided their articulation. It is possible that some document to which I have not had access does indeed contain one of these missing images. But even assuming this to be the case, I can confidently claim to have made use of at least a representative sample of available material, and this sample was devoid of such imagery. For a large representative sample to fail to give evidence of the relevant material is in itself a noteworthy and hardly coincidental fact.

In general, one can suggest four possible explanations for something important having been left unsaid: (1) it is so obvious to the audience that speaker or writer can take it as understood; (2) it is consciously suppressed by the decisionmaker so as not to conjure up disturbing associations in the mind of the audience or because it is thought to be in bad taste; (3) it is unconsciously repressed by the decisionmaker because of its personally disturbing associations; (4) decisionmakers are simply less inclined to think stereotypically in terms of analogies from recent experience than received opinion holds to be the case. While by the nature of the problem it is difficult to decide the issue definitively, on balance it seems to me that alternative 4, the most straightforward possibility, is also the likeliest.

Alternative 1 is unconvincing: when have politicians refrained from talking in platitudes or avoided certain topics merely because they were self-evident? On the contrary, one would expect familiar images to turn up frequently, certainly not to be left as understood. Alternative 2 is a possibility to be more seriously considered (and accounts for the scrupulous avoidance of the theme of the Holocaust by Israeli decisionmakers in the prelude to the 1967 war). On the other hand, one would still expect to find reference to salient images in private communications of the observer. In the cases at issue such images were absent from both public and private utterances of decisionmakers and other interested parties. Alternative 3 can less easily be dismissed than 1 and 2, if only because it is difficult to see what might count as evidence for or against it. At best one might consider it not proven and maintain an open mind about it. Either way, whether true or false, it would not contradict the validity of alternative 4 but would merely provide a more intriguing explanation for decisionmakers' avoidance of obvious analogy. In the absence of evidence or sufficient reason to the contrary, therefore, the preferred solution to the problem must tend to be the most uncomplicated.

I do not wish to claim, of course, that decisionmakers never rely upon analogies drawn from their own experience, nor that past trauma may not affect present perception. President Truman's comparison between the North Korean invasion of the South in 1950 and Nazi aggression, and Prime Minister Eden's equation of Nasser with Hitler, are both well-known, if somewhat overworked examples. Nevertheless, it can be concluded from the counterexamples studied here that analogy or historical preoccupation does not *necessarily* play a unique or even very central role in perception.

What, then, is the role of historical learning in the process of threat perception? I shall argue, in the following analysis, that *suspicion*, based upon historical experience, constitutes one of the *predispositions* influencing the observation and appraisal of evidence. But it is only a single component in an overall complex process, not, as Gosling and Jervis suggest, a linear determinant of threat perception.

Threat perception involves less an instantaneous act of recognition than a more or less protracted course of evaluation. Extending at times over several days, this process might include elements of consultation and the exercise of influence as well as reflection and analysis. This was so in 1913, 1939, and 1946. In 1875 and 1889 recognition more closely followed the receipt of specific information. Even so, this information served to confirm suspicions which had been developing over a longer period of time. It completed an overall picture rather than providing the unique cause of the recognition.

Threat perception can hardly entail simply an instantaneous act of recognition, because the perceiver was not invariably confronted with clear-cut data at once recognizable as threatening. While *perception* in its basic sense, defined above, was one component of the threat recognition—events in the external world were perceived—we cannot, without being misleading, describe the overall process as one of "perception." To arrive at a more adequate description of the phenomenon, we must recognize that in the cases reviewed here the observer defined the situation by a process of *cognitive evaluation* or judgment rather than by straightforward perception alone. Faced not so much with familiar patterns of sense-data, recognizable at once as threats, as with unfamiliar, ambiguous, and incomplete juxtapositions of signals, the meaning of which might not be readily apparent, the observer was obliged to engage in an effort, more or less protracted through time, of intellectual understanding.

This preliminary conclusion matches the description of threat perception arrived at by Richard Lazarus on the basis of research in social psychology. He argues that "threat implies a state in which the individual anticipates a confrontation with a harmful condition of some sort. Stimuli resulting in threat or non-threat reactions are cues that signify to the individual some future condition, harmful, benign or beneficial. *These and other cues are evaluated by the cognitive process of appraisal.*"[6] Furthermore, as Lazarus goes on to explain, "the appraisal of threat is not a simple perception of the elements of the situation, but a judgement, an inference in which the data are assimilated to a constellation of *ideas and expectations.*"[7]

Thus, the starting point of my analysis is the recognition that the gap between signal and reaction is filled, not by a simple perception alone, but by a process of appraisal incorporating elements both of perception (in the sense of observation) and of cognition or judgment. An argument could be made for preferring the terms *threat appraisal* or *threat assessment* to the misleading *threat perception*. But, without minimizing my reservations about the term *threat perception*, I prefer to maintain it, simply on the grounds that it is too widely accepted for its rejection at this stage to serve much purpose.

In Chapter 2 I divided the phenomenon of threat perception into four discrete stages: (1) occurrence of event, (2) perception and definition of event, (3) exploration of alternatives and choice of response, and (4) implementation of response. The focus of my interest in this study is on stage 2. My investigation of it in the following chapters falls into three parts. First, I consider those assumed conditions and salient features of the geopolitical environment within which the state was believed to function and which predisposed the observer to, or provided the background for, the perception of threat. Second, I analyze the domestic political environment within which the perceiver played out his decision-making role and which also affected his receptivity to threat. Finally—and this is the burden of my argument—I examine in detail the cognitive process of appraisal by which information was evaluated and defined as threatening. We shall then be in a position to account for the occurrence of the phenomenon.

Chapter 10

Geopolitical Environment

Threat is not perceived in a vacuum. It is neither simply a purely psychological process, unrelated to surrounding circumstances, nor, equally simplistically, the result of an objective appraisal of some unambiguous state of the environment. The perception of threat is a complex synthesis—the product of a subjective appraisal of events, selectively viewed, by decisionmakers acting within a given domestic political context, and therefore influenced and concerned by the pressures of that context, on behalf of a state actor playing out a role in a geopolitical environment believed to possess certain characteristics salient to the management of policy.

In this chapter I shall examine those aspects of the geopolitical environment, as defined by the decisionmaker, which in my judgment were important conditions for the perception of threat. From among the list of factors suggested by previous researchers and examined in my own project three sets of "predispositions" (to continue to use a term which has become generally accepted) were found to be of central significance: (a) the intense interest and involvement of the perceiver in the area at stake; (*b*) an underlying current of mistrust in relations between perceiver and perceived; and (*c*) the consciousness on the part of the perceiver of an unfavorable balance of capabilities between his own side and the perceived opponent.

Threat appraisal, as I argued in Chapter 9, can be divided into two logically distinct stages of observation and cognitive appraisal or judgment. During the period of observation the actor becomes aware of a multiplicity of outside events. As we see from our case studies, such events include newspaper articles, military preparations, diplomatic initiatives, and many other types of activity, military and nonmilitary, verbal and nonverbal. Usually no conclusion is yet drawn about the significance of such activity, except when the threatening signal is universally recognized as an indicator of impending danger; where there is no such unambiguous signal, interpretation comes at a later stage of judgment or definition of the situation.

Observation and judgment, though logically distinct, possess an important common feature: they are both psychological processes entailing a selection of material; that is, they both filter out information implicitly or explicitly considered to be irrelevant. Observation involves a selection of signals for attention from a universe of contemporary events; judgment involves a selection of explanations for those signals from a universe of possibilities. Without this filtering out or process of selection we should hardly be able to cope with incoming information. In her invaluable book *Pearl Harbor: Warning and Decision* (Stanford, 1962), Roberta Wohlstetter demonstrates how the selection of evidence at both the stage of observation and that of judgment can involuntarily remove from the attention of the actor material vital to a true perception. Thus, she points out, "to say that a signal was available is not the same as saying that it was *perceived* in the sense that it was taken as evidence or as necessitating a specific course of action in response" (p. 73). With the benefit of hindsight it is easy to know what signals should or should not have been taken into account, but at the time, information arrives without a price tag. On any single day any decisionmaker is confronted by a mass of information from many different sources and on many different subjects. In Wohlstetter's conclusions about the intelligence failure at Pearl Harbor this is one of the principal points:

> After the event, of course, a signal is always crystal-clear; we can see now what disaster it was signaling since the disaster has occurred. But before the event it is obscure and pregnant with conflicting meanings. It comes to the observer embedded in an atmosphere of "noise," i.e., in the company of all sorts of information that is useless and irrelevant for predicting the particular disaster. For example, in Washington, Pearl Harbor signals were competing with a vast number of signals from the European theater. (P. 387)

In the process of selective observation, in short, the right signals can be filtered out and the wrong signals receive attention.

Even when the right signals are observed—that is, filtered out from the background "noise"—they still have to be correctly interpreted. In the Pearl Harbor example, for instance, Japanese military preparations were understood, not as a warning of an impending attack on Hawaii, but as pointing to an impending attack on Southeast Asia. At the time, a given signal is "compatible not only with a single catastrophe, but also with many other possible outcomes" (Wohlstetter, p. 225). Sometimes, as I have already pointed out, the act of observation and the judgment of significance as a threat can be virtually simultaneous. There is no difficulty in recognizing the movement of troops on one's own border as a threat. Unfortunately many international events are less clear-cut. Whether or not a troop movement on someone else's border is to be considered a threat is not always readily apparent. Different actors will reach different conclusions about the same event. From our own case studies it can be seen that in 1913 the von Sanders mission considerably alarmed the Russian government, but British observers found it difficult at first to share in the Russian reaction. Even different officials working for the same government react differently to the same information. Wohlstetter again points out that "it was not unusual for a signal to mean one kind of danger in Washington and another in the theater" (p. 73).

Once it becomes clear that perception is essentially based on selection, first among different signals and second among competing interpretations of those signals, two leading questions present themselves: What is it that drew the attention of the observer to a particular event or signal in the first place? Why was one particular interpretation of that event preferred rather than another? Assuming that perception is not an arbitrary process, the observer presumably bases his observation and judgment, in part at least, on certain *criteria* of selection. Wohlstetter is somewhat vague about what these criteria are, though their existence is one of her primary conclusions. She refers in different places to (*a*) hypotheses that guide observation, (*b*) expectations about human behavior, and (*c*) absorption with particular geographical areas (in the Pearl Harbor example, with the European battle area) (pp. 56, 392, 230). "To discriminate significant sounds against this background of noise, one has to be listening for something or one of several things" (p. 56). Here, clearly, the stress is on factors influencing the selection of evidence. Pruitt, whose theoretical contribution to understanding threat perception is referred to in Chapter 1, would wish to complement Wohlstetter's argument by laying stress on those factors influencing the interpretation of evidence.[1] Such "predispositions" include distrust, past experience, contingency planning (that is, preoccupation with certain given possibilities), and anxiety. It can be seen that basically, Pruitt and Wohlstetter, though their examples differ, are talking about the same thing. Distrust is an expectation about human behavior; past experience provides hypotheses that guide observation; contingency planning can lead to absorption with a particular area. Although Pruitt and Wohlstetter focus on different aspects of the process of perception, the latter on the selection of evidence and the former on interpretation, I think we are justified in subsuming their perspectives (as, indeed, Knorr does) within a single framework. The present chapter will proceed to explicate those predispositions concerning the geopolitical environment which guided observation and judgment.

The most apparent predisposition to emerge from our case-studies was a geographical one. In five out of six cases—those of 1889, 1913, and 1946, and the two in 1939—the attention of decisionmakers was drawn to the events in question because they concerned or involved areas of high priority for strategic or emotional reasons or of current and urgent relevance to the observer. Only Wohlstetter, of previous researchers, has drawn attention to this factor.

Rome and the Vatican, both at the local Italian and wider international levels were—especially during the period in question (the reign of Leo XIII)—objects of the greatest interest and attention. The pope, of course, received the attention and consideration appropriate to the head of the Catholic Church. As Bishop Geremia Bonomelli wrote to Leo XIII, "With the diplomatic corps by your side, with the telegraph, with unlimited means of communication, with the moral power which you possess, with the eyes of the world always upon you, with ears always stretched to hear your words, with that illimitable, invincible publicity which accompanies your every action, you are the freest of monarchs."[2]

Most important, though, was the preoccupation at this time of Italian decisionmakers in general, and of Crispi in particular, with the Roman question. Formally, the question arose from papal refusal to recognize the legislation of 1871 that set up Rome as the capital of Italy and deprived the papacy of its temporal powers. At issue, in effect, was much more. Rome, as the symbol of past Italian greatness and present Italian rejuvenation, was a focus of nationalist aspirations. Any attempt to call into question the new status of Rome as the Italian capital—and by so eminent and influential a figure as the pope—was seen as a challenge to Italian unity and the nationalist movement. If the status of Rome had been settled and universally recognized, no problem would have arisen. This was not the case, however, and through exploitation of the Roman question, the French government could and did cause the Italians endless embarassment. As Langer says, "Italy had indeed a very vulnerable spot, and Crispi knew it only too well."[3] Moreover, the question was also bound up with the whole problem of church and state. Anticlerical provocations, such as the erection in June 1889 of a statue to Giordano Bruno, kept the issue alive and a continuing source of disquiet. Thus, Crispi's sensitivity to signals at the beginning of July 1889 concerning the position of the papacy is readily explicable and an important background factor to the perception of threat.

Danzig, like Rome, possessed both symbolic and practical importance. Situated at the mouth of the Vistula, the main Polish outlet onto the Baltic, it was of vital commercial importance. Furthermore, it was also central to Beck's vision of Poland as a Baltic and maritime power. But its primary significance derived from its historical and emotive connotations. Such considerations weighed especially heavily with Polish decisionmakers conscious, like their Italian counterparts of the late nineteenth century, of a renewed and still precarious national identity. Finally, there was the continuing tension surrounding Danzig, with a vocal and militant German population calling for their reincorporation into the Reich. Despite periodic German assurances problems concerning Polish rights in the Free Port continued to crop up regularly throughout the late thirties. Local incidents and demonstrations against Poland were frequent and served to maintain Polish vigilance. When, therefore, the issue was first raised by the German government in October 1938 Beck reàcted firmly and rapidly. In his instructions to Lipski, the Polish ambassador in Berlin, Beck stressed the vital nature of Danzig at length and in all its aspects: historical, geographic, commercial, maritime, legal, and most important, political. The Danzig question was "a sure criterion for estimating the German Reich's intentions towards Poland." Beck emphasized that "any attempt to incorporate the Free City into the Reich, must inevitably lead to conflict."[4] Despite his clear-cut refusal to alter the status of the port, the German government continued to press for negotiations during Beck's visit to Berlin in January and that of Ribbentrop to Warsaw in February 1939. On the eve of the German entry into Prague, the Danzig question was both a live issue and one certain to arouse Polish disquiet. Danzig, in short, was a very sensitive topic.

Russian decisionmakers, in their turn, were highly vigilant to signals concerning the status of Constantinople and the Straits. As with Rome and Danzig, Constantinople was both emotively and historically salient, and politically problematic. In the context of a disintegrating Ottoman Empire the future of Constantinople was as uncertain as it was crucial. That concern for Constantinople and the Turkish Straits was uppermost in the minds of Russian decisionmakers is apparent from the Sazonov memorandum of 6 December 1913, in which it was forcefully argued that any state in possession of the Straits would acquire the strength of a great power by virtue of the area's exceptional geographical advantages. It would hold the key to the Black Sea and the Mediterranean; it would have the means of penetrating into Asia Minor and of achieving hegemony in the Balkans; it would be in a position to retrace the historical steps taken by the Turks in their time.[5] Little wonder, therefore, that events in the Turkish capital were followed with great interest. "You know how sensitive we are about Constantinople,"Sazonov commented to the French ambassador in November 1912.[6] During the Liman von Sanders crisis the point was constantly reiterated: "Everything that transpires in Constantinople is of the highest importance for Russia."[7] A German command would have been acceptable anywhere else but in the Turkish capital. In his memoirs Sazonov made much of the point: Bethmann-Hollweg should have known "that if there was any point in the world upon which our attention was jealously concentrated, and where we could not permit any changes directly concerning our vital interests, that point was certainly Constantinople, which controlled our access to the Mediterranean—the natural outlet of the trade of Southern Russia."[8]

By coincidence, the 1946 crisis also arose in part from

sensitivity to developments in the Turkish Straits area. This should not be too surprising when one considers that this passage of water connecting the Black Sea to the Mediterranean has been a focus of international interest for at least two centuries. If on the Russian side there has long been a keen desire to achieve unrestricted access for warships and cargo boats to the Mediterranean—while restricting foreign access to the Black Sea—other great powers have traditionally sought to oppose Russian ambitions for fear of Russian domination of the Eastern Mediterranean and even beyond. Thus in 1946 we find American decisionmakers highly alert to the strategic significance of the Straits area and determined to prevent Soviet Russia from obtaining the supposedly wide-ranging advantages to be gained from their control. Acheson narrates a significant anecdote of the key policy meeting of 15 August 1946: "The President took out from the drawer of his desk a large map of the Middle East and Eastern Mediterranean and asked us to gather around behind him. He then gave us a brief lecture on the strategic importance of the area and the extent to which we must be prepared to keep it free from Soviet domination."[9]

In previous cases the area under surveillance was not only a focus of interest in a generalized sense, but also tended (though not in 1913) to be a live political issue in the period preceding the ultimate crisis. This was so in 1946. Since March 1945, when the Soviet Union had denounced its treaty of neutrality and nonaggression with Turkey, the USSR had exerted continuous pressure for border changes and a revision of the Montreux Convention. Published American documents indicate that the U.S. government followed the development of the dispute with great interest and increasing concern. In November 1945, in the spirit of the agreement at Potsdam, the United States presented detailed suggestions for a revision of the Montreux Convention to the Turkish government. Then between January and May 1946 a revealing change occurred in the American sense of involvement with the issue. In January 1946 the Turkish foreign minister, Hasan Saka, was obliged to explain the nature of Soviet claims to Secretary of State Byrnes.[10] By May, Byrnes was openly reassuring the Turkish ambassador in Paris that if in the past the United States had perhaps not known Turkey and Turkey's problems very well, she was now well posted concerning Turkey, took a great interest in Turkey's problems, and had a real and sincere friendship for her.[11] When the Soviet proposals for a revision of the Montreux Convention were finally presented in August 1946, they were unlikely to be received with anything but the greatest attention in Washington.

The case of Britain in March 1939 possesses certain points of resemblance to that of the United States in 1946. There was no traditional or sentimental British interest in Czechoslovakia in particular or in Central and Eastern Europe in general. On the contrary, France had failed for years to draw Britain into some kind of involvement in the area. The 1925 Locarno treaties had, to France's chagrin, limited Britain's commitment to a defense of the integrity of the states on Germany's western borders and had been eloquently silent about her eastern frontiers. Had Chamberlain not expressed British indifference to Czechoslovakia at the time of Munich in those famous words "How horrible, fantastic, incredible it is that we should be digging trenches and trying on gas-masks here because of a quarrel in a far-away country between people of whom we know nothing"? Then after Munich the British government had more or less written off Central and Southeastern Europe to the German sphere of influence.

Despite the apparent absence of a British interest in the area or a sense of its strategic importance, the fate of Czechoslovakia was bound, after Munich, to compel attention. Britain, like the United States in 1946, could hardly avoid a close and vigilant surveillance of what had become one of the most relevant and pressing issues of the period. The salience, in spite of a lack of historical commitment, of the Czechoslovak issue for Britain finds straightforward expression in the sheer volume of contemporary analysis devoted to it in the press and other publications, intelligence reports, diplomatic documents, and cabinet papers. Here was an area that simply could not be overlooked.

A second geopolitical factor making for extreme sensitivity to threatening signals in three out of the six cases—those of 1875, 1889, and 1946—was an atmosphere of tension and mistrust in ongoing relations between the observed and observing actors. This sort of relationship has aptly been called a "bad-faith model," implying a continuing interaction of mutual suspicion and fear, and a high state of vigilance on both sides to the least hint of aggressive intentions.[12] Both in observation and in judgment actors display an incorrigible suspicion of each other; that is, they are, at one and the same time, highly alert to any sign of hostility and inclined to judge any word or act, once observed, in the worst possible light. Thus the case studies here confirm the existence of one of the primary predispositional factors proposed by Singer and Pruitt.

The most patent example of the bad-faith model is provided by the Cold War between the Soviet Union and the United States. No matter how one analyzes and describes the origins of the Cold War, it has become clear, with the publication of the relevant American documents for 1946, that by the spring and summer of that year Soviet-American relations had locked into a vicious circle of hostility and mistrust.[13] Wherever Soviet and American interests came into contact—in Manchuria, Korea, Trieste, Germany, or the Near East—wartime cooperation (or at least communication) had broken down to be replaced by abrasive and hostile disagreement. In the dynamic of deteriorating relations between the two states which characterized the early stages of the Cold War, Iran and Turkey played a central role, for this was the one area, along the whole length of the European and Near Eastern borders of the Soviet Union where governments not subservient to Moscow remained in power.

The scare of March 1946, which arose from information about Soviet troop movements towards the Iranian border, both expressed and intensified American vigilance to and suspicion of Soviet intentions in the Near East; sufficient to note Truman's remark to Harriman at the time that the United States might soon be at war with the Soviet Union over Iran.[14] Given an American assumption of bad faith on the part of the Soviet Union, it was only a short step to the conclusion that the latter wished to extend its area of domination to take in Iran and Turkey. When the Soviet Union presented its proposals on the Straits to Turkey in August 1946, these were quickly seen in Washington as evidence of expansive intent.

While the term itself is an anachronism, it is surely not inappropriate to describe Franco-German relations following the war of 1870 as a further classic example of a cold war situation, in which there was a dialectic of hostility, suspicion, and vigilance. The series of minor alarms that preceded the major war scare of 1875 reflected an underlying and continuous French anxiety about German intentions and an extreme sensitivity to minimal evidence of hostile action. The slightest nuance of tone or detail was picked up and analyzed with attention and concern by French decisionmakers. For instance, in April 1872 the delayed return of the German ambassador to his post in Paris was considered extremely disquieting; perhaps some kind of veiled threat was intended.[15] In July 1874 Decazes argued that the mere anxiety of the English Prince of Wales about Franco-German relations deserved to be taken seriously. There was a need, he informed his representatives throughout Europe, for ever-continuing vigilance to any symptoms which might illuminate Germany's future intentions.[16] Vigilance was thus incorporated into the "operating code" of the French Foreign Service.

In the 1875 crisis itself an assumption of German malevolence is apparent throughout. Whatever reassurance might be given to Decazes, he remained suspicious and tense. For instance, on 5 April 1875, when Decazes admitted to Lord Lyons that his personal relations with the German ambassador were quite friendly and that he had received no official complaints from the German government, his conclusion from this was not that there was no cause for concern, but that, on the contrary, this might merely be the lull before the storm.

It was "the sort of treatment applied by Churchmen to sin-
ners who were supposed to be sure to die in final impeni-
tence."[17] Even this imagery, of a sinner irrevocably condemned to eternal damnation, is surely expressive. Such
deep-seated and almost intangible dread of German retribu-
tion was clearly an important precondition of the 1875 war
scare. French unease neither began (nor ended) with the affair but was a constant accompaniment to Franco-German relations in this period.

    In the 1889 case a similar relationship of sensitivity and
suspicion existed between France and Italy, though it was
felt especially intensely on the Italian side. Relations between the two states steadily worsened after Crispi's arrival
to power and were not improved by mutual polemics in
press and parliament. As with the two previous examples a
history of incidents and alarms provided a prelude to the major scare under investigation. Crispi, personally, became a
byword in diplomatic circles for suspiciousness and alarmism. The slightest rumor seemed to touch off an urgent request for assistance in Berlin, Vienna, or London. Thus, when
at the beginning of June 1889 an obscure incident took place
involving, as the French inquiry revealed, an Italian barque
found in possession of contraband, the affair became "the
subject of much excited comment in Italy" and brought a renewal of tension between the two countries.[18] In the context
of a more confident relationship such an incident would
quickly have blown over. In the bad-faith model the significance of the event was exaggerated and seen as evidence of
some sinister design. The ultimate invasion scare of July
1889 can be understood only in terms of a framework of suspicious expectation into which "evidence" of French hostility was readily assimilated. Without ignoring certain indications of Crispi's personal instability and "eccentricity" (see
Chapter 11, below), it almost seems as though the bad-faith
model created an anticipation of some hostile act by France.
In any event, France was seen to be playing out a role already assigned to it by the observer. Called back to Rome by
the scare, Giolitti, the finance minister, attempted to reason

with Crispi that France could obtain no possible advantage from an attack on Italy. But Giolitti, along with some other doubters, was in a minority. Crispi "remained unshaken in his conviction, as if he had no doubt about the matter."[19]

In these three examples of the bad-faith model, the stress is on the ongoing nature of the hostile relationship. Thus, the threat perception in each fitted into a continuing pattern of ill-will and incident which both influenced the selection of evidence and biased its interpretation. In our other three cases, those of 1913 and the two from 1939, the relationship between the actors was more ambivalent. On the one hand, there was no bad-faith model or framework of expectation into which selected evidence was fitted; on the other hand, a more or less recent history of wariness and dispute over particular issues had left a residue of unease and a climate of opinion which, at the appropriate moment, influenced the judgment of the observer and contributed to the perception of threat. Put in another way, the bad-faith model defines the observed actor as an enemy, while the second, or "minor," model defines the observed actor as a potential opponent to be treated with caution.

Russo-German relations, for example, had been marked, long before November 1913, by mistrust and periodic tension. At the turn of the century Russian suspicion of German penetration into Asia Minor was aroused by the Baghdad Railway scheme for building a line from the Sea of Marmara to the Persian Gulf. At the time the Russian foreign minister declared in a memorandum to the czar that Russia could not allow attempts on the part of Germany "to play a preponderant role on the banks of the Bosphorus, where we have unchallangeable historical tasks."[20] In 1911 Germany and Russia concluded negotiations by which Russia agreed to cease opposition to construction of the railway in return for German recognition of Northern Persia as a Russian sphere of influence. But recent research in the czarist archives indicates that Sazonov was prompted to make the agreement precisely in order to ensure Russia's military security in the Caucasus and Black Sea area in the face of what were seen as German imperial ambitions. Declining British interest in the railway and successful German penetration into the Near East compelled Sazonov to make the best of a difficult situation.[21] Nor was the possibility of a war between these two members of opposing alliances ever far-fetched. In September 1908 an incident involving German deserters from the French Foreign Legion created an atmosphere in which Izvolski, the Russian foreign minister, fearing war with Germany, sought assurance from the English ambassador that England would stand by France. Meanwhile, the Russian military attaché in Berlin noted that Germany believed the time was opportune for a Russo-German war.[22] Only a few months later the Bosnian crisis placed the Russian government in a position in which it was compelled by a virtual German ultimatum to withdraw its support for Serbia.

Against this evidence of a history of tension in Russo-German relations and Russian suspicion of German aims in Asia Minor—with war a contingency to be taken into account, if only in military planning—we must juxtapose the cautious improvement in relations after 1911, culminating in Sazonov's friendly conversation in Berlin in October 1913 with Bethmann-Hollweg. When, therefore, news of the von Sanders mission reached Sazonov in the first week of November 1913, he reacted with surprise and consternation. Here the contrast with Decazes, Crispi, and Truman is especially marked, since these decisionmakers had been expecting a hostile move by the opponent. Nonetheless, the threatening significance of the new mission to Constantinople was quickly grasped, partly because of a general sensitivity to events in the area, but also because the signal could be accommodated to long-held suspicions of German ambitions.

A very similar situation existed in the case of Britain in March 1939: an improved atmosphere in relations with Germany on the eve of the crisis, together with a history of tension and suspicion. Throughout the winter of 1938–39 the German press was filled with anti-British abuse. On 25 January 1939 the post-Munich deterioration in Anglo-German relations had reached the point where Halifax could bring before the Cabinet evidence of an impending German adventure in the spring either against the East or against the West. Not even the possibility of a sudden air attack on England could be ruled out, to be followed by land and sea operations against the Western Powers. "Hitler's mental condition, his insensate rage against Great Britain and his megalomania," the foreign secretary reported, "which are alarming the moderates around him, are entirely consistent with the execution of a desperate coup against the Western powers."[23] Speaking in Parliament on 6 February 1939, Chamberlain declared "that any threat to the vital interests of France from whatever quarter it came must evoke the immediate cooperation of this country."[24] Yet with the return of Henderson to his Berlin post and the renewal of Anglo-German commercial contacts, the air seemed to clear somewhat. At the beginning of March 1939 Chamberlain had an optimistic off-the-record chat with the press, while Hoare made his notorious "Golden Age" speech. There *were* reports, first of possible German "pressure" on Czechoslovakia, then, from intelligence sources on 11 March 1939, of an impending German invasion. These do not seem to have been taken especially seriously. Halifax recorded on 13 March "a negative improvement in the situation, in that rumours and scares have died down, and it is not plain that the German Government are planning mischief in any particular quarter. (I hope they may not be taking, even as I write, an unhealthy interest in the Slovak situation!)"[25] Thus, on the very eve of the crisis, and despite available signs, there was no expectation of an imminent German move against Britain or inimicable to British interests. Unlike the bad-faith model, there was no selective perception. When the blow fell, however, and German troops entered Prague in breach of the Munich Agreement and all assurances, the open-minded among British decision-makers (Chamberlain constitutes a special problem; see Chapter 11, below) quickly concluded that here was confirmation of German expansive ambitions. Hore-Belisha expressed the view that the German move was the beginning of the *Drang Nach Osten*.[26] Halifax also was soon talking of a

German plot to "dominate Europe and, if possible, the world."
Cadogan, permanent under secretary at the Foreign Office,
noted revealingly in his diary: "I always said that, as long as
Hitler could pretend he was incorporating Germans in the
Reich, *we could pretend* that he had a case. If he proceeded
to gobble up other nationalities, that would be the time to
call 'Halt!'"[27] He was saying, in effect, that he had suspected
all along that German aims were not limited to the redress of
specific grievances. As in the 1913 case, German actions
could rapidly be accommodated to a latent model of German
behavior, in this case and in Hore-Belisha's words, the *Drang
Nach Osten.*

The same ambivalence to the opponent found in the Russian and British examples is exemplified in the Polish case.
Here again there were traditional reasons why Polish decisionmakers should be on their guard against German hostility: Polish public opinion was incurably ill-disposed towards
Germany; German rearmament would seem to pose a natural
danger to Poland; the situation in Danzig, a central issue between the two states, never ceased to be difficult and tense.
In Debicki's words, "the dynamism and ruthlessness of Nazism, introduced into the Free City's domestic policy, were
by their very nature opposed to Polish interests and aims."[28]
To these primary sources of mistrust can be added other aspects of Polish-German relations which, although not exaggerated at the time, seemed to Lipski, looking back on the
crisis, "to evoke an understandable mistrust and criticism":
German activities in Slovakia "hostile to Poland" and, more
ominous, support by the SS and Gestapo for the Ukrainian
separatist movement.[29] Yet, until Prague, both Beck and Hitler
made the effort to maintain a proper relationship, and Beck
was prepared to overlook Nazi activism over the Danzig and
Ukrainian questions as the work of party extremists.[30] Indeed,
most of the concrete problems that arose concerning, for example, Polish Jews resident in Germany, Polish rights in
Danzig, or the minorities question were resolved successfully, despite invariable tension and abrasion at popular and
junior official levels. Even when, to Beck's dismay, first Rib-

bentrop and then Hitler in person raised the question of re-
negotiating the status of Danzig, Beck still remained
convinced that at the very highest level Poland and Germany
possessed complementary interests. The fundamental antagonism between German Nazism and Soviet Communism,
he believed, made Poland far too important a potential ally
to Germany for something like the Danzig issue to be allowed to disrupt relations. Hence, until the crisis Beck continued to interpret German policy as not essentially directed
against Poland. He told Gafencu on 2 March 1939: "If they
touch Danzig, it means war. But why should they touch it,
since the fate of this city can always be settled amicably between Germany and ourselves?"[31]

Like Sazonov in 1913, Beck reacted to the German declaration of a protectorate over Slovakia with surprise and consternation precisely because it did not fit his preconceived
image of German intentions. For several days, in fact, he continued to cling to a somewhat wishful view of the situation,
in contrast to Polish public opinion, which had no difficulty
in at once perceiving a threat to Poland. Then, when Ribbentrop raised the Danzig question again, this time in a less-
than-friendly tone, Beck quickly adjusted his views to conform with public opinion. His more "sophisticated" image of
a Germany concerned to maintain good relations with Poland was replaced by a more traditional "folk" image of a
hostile Germany opposed to an independent Poland.

A final geopolitical factor to be considered relates to the
confidence of the observer in his basic defensive potential
against the perceived opponent. Both Singer and Pruitt, as I
noted in Chapter 1, argue that "estimated capability" is one
of the main conditions underlying the perception of an opponent as threatening. While neither author fully defines or
develops the concept, I take it to mean the estimated capability of the opponent to implement the perceived threat.
What this formulation overlooks is that capability is not an
absolute. The relevant factor is not the capability of the opponent in isolation but the general confidence of the observer in his ability to confront and overcome a dangerous

challenge should it arise. This version comes much closer to what Lazarus, treating threat in a social-psychological frame-work, calls the "relative balance of power between the harm-producing stimulus to be confronted and the counterharm resources of the individual and the environment."[32] The ad-vantage of this formulation is that it takes in other than straightforward military considerations and forces one to consider additional factors such as morale, political exper-tise, and stability, as well as factors in the geopolitical envi-ronment such as diplomatic position, aid from alliance partners, and so on. Moreover, not all threats are directed against the security of the actor but can involve questions of prestige, economy, and overall strategic situation. A great power, with extensive commitments and a sprawling, devel-oped economy, can be every bit as sensitive to threat, seen from this point of view, as a small power with far fewer re-sources but also without the burden of far-reaching commit-ments. What is important is the actor's sense of security and belief in his capability of meeting such problems as might arise. This is not to suggest that confidence can be a substi-tute for resources when the actor is put to the test, but rather that the psychological factor will influence the actor's sensi-tivity in anticipating danger.

In five out of our six cases an important condition in the perception of threat was the observer's sense of vulnerability to the given opponent in the area threatened. In three out of those five cases the threat perceived conformed to an exist-ing obsession derived from this sense of vulnerability. This strongly duplicates Bialer's finding that one of the primary factors underlying the interwar British obsession with aerial bombardment—the "Luftwaffe complex"—was a conviction in the absolute vulnerability of Britain's cities.[33] On the other hand, the evidence here tends to disprove a Jervis proposi-tion associating vulnerability with the denial of threat.*

Serious French resistance in 1875 to a German offensive

---

* "If there is nothing a person can do to avoid the pain that accompanies a stimulus, his perceptual threshold for the stimulus will be raised (defense). If, on the other hand, he can avoid the pain by recognizing the stimulus and

was, as the army and political leadership well knew, more than hopeless; it was impossible. Only two years after the end of the German occupation France had no army to match that of Germany and no allies to correct the imbalance. France's eastern border with Germany was defended by one army corps, five regiments, and two cavalry divisions, all of which were understrength; the infantry was in the middle of being reequipped; the Territorial Army existed only on paper, and its senior officers had not yet been appointed. As for fortifications, plans had been drawn up in detail, but work on them had only just commenced. Finally, no contingency plans existed for German attacks through Belgium or Switzerland, nor, in fact, were contingency plans available for the retreat beyond the Loire mentioned by Decazes to Orlov. In contrast to this sorry picture, French intelligence estimated that in the event of war Germany could put into battle 130,000 men in three weeks and 600,000 combatants altogether.[34] Not surprising, therefore, that the British military attaché in Paris did "not know a single sensible officer of any standing in the services who does not think that a war within two years, in which France would have to act single-handed, must end in calamity."[35] Nor, indeed, in the light of French defenselessness, is it at all surprising that French decisionmakers should have been quite so alert to the least sign of German attack. Were such an attack to come, they had no hope by themselves of avoiding defeat, occupation, and reparation.

If French vigilance is not difficult to account for, the weakness of the French Army cannot in itself explain the obsession with invasion reflected in the war scare of 1875 and the alarms which preceded it. To be alert is one thing; to be convinced beyond argument that the opponent is merely waiting for his moment to attack, quite another. This "invasion psychosis," as one author calls it,[36] found expression at all levels of public opinion, from the presidency downwards. Ample evidence of the obsession is found in contemporary

---

taking corrective action, his threshold will be lowered" (R. Jervis, *Perception and Misperception in International Politics* [Princeton, 1976], p. 373).

literature and the press.[37] Its roots, I would suggest, lay in the
traumatic experience of "the terrible year" of 1870—a year
of invasion and defeat, followed by a humiliating occupation
that left deep and lasting scars on the French national consciousness. Now a trauma, in the psychiatric sense, is a startling experience that has a lasting effect on mental life; unable
to master it or discharge its effects, the subject returns again
and again to relive the original shocking experience. He will,
moreover, live in constant fear of its repetition. Analogously,
those Frenchmen who had lived through the disaster of 1870
and after continued to be obsessed by a fear of the repetition
of the original trauma. When to this collective obsession is
added the total incapacity of the group to overcome the pro-
jected threat, should it arise, we arrive at the fearful and de-
moralized situation of the French nation in the years following
the German occupation. No failure of the threat to actually
materialize could alter the French conviction that at some
time the invasion would take place. Hence, Decazes, faced
by evidence that Germany was unlikely to attack France in
1875, still maintained that Germany would invade "not perhaps tomorrow, but at some, probably not distant moment,
which is as yet undefined and . . . crush [France] forever."[38]
Avoidance of such an attack was the central aim of French
policy.[39]

Crispi and the Italian Admiralty were almost equally preoccupied, as we saw in Chapter 4, with the possibility of a
surprise French naval attack on the Italian coast. While we
cannot trace this fear back to any specific historical trauma, it
first began to appear in the wake of the scare of February–
March 1888. It may be, of course, that this scare did have a
traumatic effect on Crispi, but neither his diaries nor the
published documents permit such a conclusion to be put forward with any degree of confidence.

In overall terms the strength of the Triple Alliance and
the various surrounding agreements made a French attack
suicidal by any rational calculation. No such rational calculation was made, though Crispi, apparently aware of this, did
attempt to *rationalize* his judgment. France, he argued, was

"full of illusions" as to her strength and convinced of her "invincibility." In this way Crispi could maintain consistency by arguing for the opponent's irrationality. Whatever might happen in the latter stages of a war with France, when the Triple Alliance could bring its massive superiority to bear, Crispi was uniquely conscious of the naval shortcomings of the alliance in the short term. Rather than being encouraged by its advantages, Crispi was preoccupied with its single, if admitted, point of weakness. He was haunted by the image of the Italian Fleet destroyed at its moorings at La Spezia, the smoking ruins of unfortified coastal towns, and an Italy torn apart by subsequent civil insurrection. It was this sense of vulnerability—no matter how irrational—that laid the groundwork for the July 1889 invasion scare. The example thus stresses both the subjective and the selective nature of confidence.

British weakness in 1939 was certainly not imagined or exaggerated: neither the military nor the diplomatic resources existed to face up to the German threat. As the Chiefs of Staff had reported in January 1939, the ultimate outcome of a conflict involving Britain might depend on the intervention of the United States—a dismaying prognostication, since the United States remained aloof from international entanglements. In the aftermath of Prague, Britain was left with no alternative but to patch together some kind of diplomatic front to German expansion and to press ahead, with renewed haste, with rearmament. The link with 1875 and 1889 exists in Chamberlain's obsession with fears of a sudden German air attack, shared, as Bialer demonstrates, by many in British public life.

Munich had revealed the serious inadequacies of Britain's air defenses—a daunting lack of fighters, antiaircraft guns, searchlights, or radar. Germany, it was believed, enjoyed overwhelming air superiority and a faster rate of aircraft production. In the event of war, Chamberlain and his colleagues envisaged London's being almost immediately devastated by air attacks, against which the known means of defense, even should they be available, would be painfully vulnerable. This view, widely held by the military, was summed up by General Ironside in his diary at the time of Munich: "Chamberlain is of course right. We have not the means of defending ourselves and he knows it . . . we simply cannot expose ourselves now to a German attack. We simply commit suicide if we do."[40] Fear of air attack was in no way lessened by the Munich Settlement, as we see from the scare of January 1939. Intelligence of a possible preemptive German air strike was taken very seriously indeed by Halifax and the Foreign Office. In the March crisis itself we have the evidence of the minister for war, Hore-Belisha, for the critical influence of the obsession. British policy, he admitted to Liddell Hart, "was dominated in any crisis by fear of the effects of London being bombed." On 22 March, following the annexation of Memel, Chamberlain wanted to mobilize the Air Defence of Great Britain and was aghast when told that it would take twelve hours to get the Anti-aircraft Territorials in position.[41] Hore-Belisha was presumably suggesting that no adequate reason existed to call such a state of alert; certainly none of the extensive available sources give even a hint of any concrete grounds for taking such a step.

What neither Chamberlain nor anyone else at the time seems to have realized was "that the Luftwaffe could only attack England effectively after the German army had conquered France and Belgium."[42] Otherwise German aircraft simply did not have the range to carry out such a mission and return home. And who could have imagined at this time that the French Army, on paper the strongest in Europe, would be unable to withstand a German assault? Nor, in fact, did the Luftwaffe even have a doctrine of strategic bombing or plans for a knock-out blow.[43] Partly, one supposes, these oversights arose from inadequate or misleading intelligence. But they also arose from a significant reluctance to examine rationally the assumptions underlying strategic bombing. "Our belief in the bomber was intuitive," confessed Marshall of the Royal Air Force Sir John Slessor in his memoirs, "a matter of faith."[44] In short, British fears of air attack, which had such an important influence on British perceptions and policy throughout the period, were not based on any rational analysis of the strategic situation. Like Crispi, British decision-makers were obsessed with their point of greatest weakness without submitting their fears to a searchingly critical analysis. In the 1913 and 1946 cases we are not faced with an obsession about insecurity, as in the cases considered above, but in both cases a sense of vulnerability to the opponent in the area threatened was an important precondition of threat perception.

Russian vulnerability in the 1913 von Sanders affair was both diplomatic and military. There were few sanctions which could be brought to bear either in Constantinople or in Berlin. When the Turks had retaken Adrianople from the Bulgarians the previous July, Sazonov had conspicuously failed to coordinate with the other Great Powers pressure on the Porte to end this intervention.[45] At the same time it had emerged that Russia was incapable of sending an expeditionary force against Turkey in the Black Sea area. Well might the British chargé d'affaires in St. Petersburg describe Sazonov's posture at the end of November 1913 as one "merely of impotent annoyance. He says he has used strong language at Berlin. What good will that do?"[46] Sazonov drew the appropriate conclusions from this revelation of impotence. His memorandum of 6 December to the czar called for a special conference to study the measures by which Russian military and naval power in the Black Sea might be augmented. Irrespective of whether Russia could fight a general war or not, local weakness had exposed her to a serious diplomatic defeat.

A similar predicament faced the United States in 1946—local vulnerability in an area of great strategic importance. The United States found itself faced with a Soviet "offensive" in an area "where the Soviets' physical position was strongest and that of the United States weakest."[47] Both in the air and on the ground the Soviet Union possessed overwhelming superiority. The United States Navy, the strongest of the services in relation to the Soviet Union, was at "a dangerously low point of efficiency" because of rapid demobilization. Hence Forrestal's apprehension in August 1946 that the United States would be unable "to meet any sudden emergency in Europe."[48] At the opening of any hostilities with the Soviet Union, the administration had been informed by the Joint Chiefs of Staff, the Red Army could conquer much, and perhaps all, of continental Western Europe. The earliest U.S. response would be strategic air attacks upon vital areas of the USSR.[49]

There is one important exception to the pattern associating the perception of threat with a prior sense of vulnerability—a reminder that there are no immutable "laws" governing the behavior of actors in the international system even when the causal connection seems almost self-evident. In the case of Poland in March 1939, Polish decisionmakers perceived the threat of a German attack while simultaneously expressing their contempt for German strength. Beck argued, for instance, that the Germans were marching across Europe with nine divisions. Poland would not be overcome by such forces and had arrived at a difficult moment with all the trump cards in her hand. Nor was Beck's a solitary voice. Gluchowski, Polish deputy minister for war, was reported to have stated in a serious conversation that "the German Wehrmacht was a great bluff, since Germany lacked the trained reserves to maintain standards. On the question whether he believed that Poland was more than a match militarily for Germany, Gluchowski answered: 'But naturally.'"[50] Given the collapse of the Polish Army in September 1939, it is difficult for the contemporary reader to believe that the Poles could ever have been confident in their armed strength. By all "objective" standards the Polish Army, certainly compared with the German Army, was an inadequate fighting force, deficient in all branches of modern warfare. But the essential point is that these deficiencies were not recognized by the Poles themselves at the time. Strategically, the army was dominated by outdated and inappropriate ideas. Any future conflict, it was believed, would follow the pattern of the Polish-Soviet war of 1920, in which horse cavalry had played a major part. No independent striking role was envisaged for either the air force or the armored corps.[51] From the point of view of intelligence, Poland persistently underestimated German strength. The Polish Deuxième Bureau failed to detect the main body of German reserves and also had insufficient knowledge of German plans for mobilization. Even then Smigly-Rydz, the inspector-general of the armed forces, considered intelligence estimates as exaggerated.[52] When eventually war came, it was met by enthusiasm in the army, and such was the confidence of Poland's leaders that they refused to bring the opposition parties into a government of national unity. They had "no intention of sharing the victory with anyone."[53]

If Germany was believed to be in a weaker position than Poland, then a Polish perception of threat would, according to common sense, be a sort of contradiction in terms: to be afraid of an opponent whom you are confident of defeating. Yet this contradiction is more apparent than real. One can perceive war to be a threat, even though one is confident of victory, because even a successful war is a damaging and unpleasant affair. Beck himself was conscious of another kind of contradiction: if Germany was weaker than Poland, would it not be irrational for her to launch an attack? His own explanation was to argue that Germany could no longer be counted on to act rationally: "This enemy constitutes an embarassing factor; he seems in effect to have lost all proportion in his thinking and action."[54] Ultimately, whether or not the Polish threat perception was logically inconsistent is irrelevant, since the threat was not based on logic. Nevertheless, a most interesting and significant point is that very soon after the scare of March 1939 Polish opinion began to cease to take seriously the possibility of a German attack. In the Polish press German military preparations were presented as a "war of nerves" and a bluff. Hitler, it was argued, would hesitate before attacking a strong Poland allied to France and England. This attitude was shared by the Foreign Ministry, the government, and even by Smigly-Rydz, who, of all people, should have known better. At a meeting of the Polish government on 11 August 1939 Smigly-Rydz argued that there would be no war that year—"autumn would pass peacefully"—and that information received of a German attack (including detailed operational plans) had been leaked deliberately to mislead them.[55] All of this strongly suggests that in most cases a sense of vulnerability is a precondition of perceiving threat and that where this is not the case the observer finds it difficult to maintain his sense of anxiety. Only in the short term is it possible to preserve the contradiction that one fears an enemy attack at the same time that one is confident of one's superiority.*

---

* Poland's overconfidence and dismissal of German military capability, its attachment to outdated strategic doctrines, and the failure of its intelligence service are all strongly reminiscent of the factors believed to underlie Israel's failure to perceive an Egyptian threat on the eve of the 1973 Yom Kippur War.

Chapter 11

Domestic Political Environment

Just as conditions in the geopolitical environment affect the perception of threat, so can the circumstances of the domestic political environment. Charles Lockhart stresses the influence of domestic political pressures on decisionmakers' perceptions. Klaus Knorr argues that the structure and assumptions of the decisionmaking group, the relevant bureaucracy, or the regime in general can importantly affect the appraisal of a given observer. He also emphasizes, as do Steinberg and Pruitt, the role of personal attitudes and traits in the process of perception.[1]

The problem I seek to tackle in this chapter is a twofold one: first, whether and which internal factors did affect the perception of threat in the case studies under consideration; and second, and rather more difficult, the extent to which one factor rather than another was operative in any given instance. Was the sensitivity to threat of a certain decisionmaker explicable on the grounds of individual personality traits or, say, the flexibility of bureaucratic procedures? Was there, perhaps, an element of interaction between the factors, a sort of "amplification" effect?

Outside the ideal conditions of the laboratory, theoretically discrete variables such as personality traits, public opinion, and political structure do not necessarily allow of a separate and differentiated treatment. One type of personality, for example, is likely to be more at home in an authoritarian regime or an especially closed-minded bureaucracy, than another. Similarily, receptivity to threat and receptivity to surrounding opinion may be thought to be correlated. A final example might be a link between the effectiveness of the pressure of public opinion and the openness of the regime to dissent. Other links and interconnections could easily be postulated.

It is this apparent interweaving of the varied domestic influences on perception that justifies a coordinated approach within a single chapter. Equally, the analyst cannot avoid the attempt to evaluate the relative weight of the different variables.

My initial task, therefore, is to provide a set of indicators of the working of the different factors. In other words we must consider which clues or criteria could permit detection of the various influences on the perception of threat.

1. We can postulate that the personality of the observer is an operative factor in the perception of threat in the presence of one of the following conditions:

(*a*)   When the initial perception of the observer is in marked contrast to that widely held within the decisionmaking group and, to a lesser extent, to opinion outside that group. (The latter divergence carries less weight since "outsiders" do not necessarily possess the same specialized information available to "insiders.")

(*b*)   When the sensitivity or the insensitivity of the observer to threatening signals is in marked contrast to that of the surrounding decisionmaking group,

(*c*)   When, failing *a* and *b*, in the judgment of the researcher, the observer displays exaggerated sensitivity or insensitivity to threatening signals. This criterion is not ideal from a scientific point of view, since the researcher himself hardly constitutes a contemporary basis of comparison. As long as the limitations of this criterion are understood, however, the greater flexibility it provides may be desirable for two reasons: first, because of the absence of sufficient evidence on a control group (i.e., surrounding decisionmakers), and second, because of the possibility that the principal decisionmaker has surrounded himself with colleagues compliant with his attitudes.

Conversely, the personality of the observer could not be considered a relevant factor in the perception of threat were the individual to conform, *from the outset*, to the opinion prevailing within the decisionmaking group. It may be that even in these circumstances personality does indeed exercise an influence on the perception of the observer. But in the absence of any indicator, the researcher is not in a position to express a considered judgment on the matter.

Finally, if personality is an operative factor in perception, it will be of interest to see whether the observer's behavior can be related to any known theories relating particular personality traits or types to receptivity to threat.

2. We can deduce the influence of public opinion on the perception of decisionmakers in the event that the latter adjust their *initial* perception of the situation, in response to pressure, in the direction of that prevailing either within the decisionmaking group or among the public at large. In order to demonstrate the existence of a causal connection, we would have to show that there is evidence

(*a*)   of an initial discrepancy between the perception of the individual decisionmaker and that of the group or of the public;

(*b*)   of the exercise or perceived exercise of pressure on the divergent observer to conform to the alternative perception;

(*c*)   of a shift in the perception of the divergent observer away from his initial position;

(*d*)   of the saliency of *b* on *c*.

3. The influence of the third domestic factor, the nature of the political system, on the perception of observers, is much more difficult to detect within the context of the present study than those referred to already. Ideally, evidence on the subject would be obtained by comparing the extent to which decisionmakers in states $A, B, C, \ldots$ of political structure X consistently differed in their assessments of a range of given threatening situations from their counterparts in states $L, M, N, \ldots$ of political structure Y. Unfortunately, this sort of rigorous investigation is not feasible here, for several reasons: first, we are examining unique situations, rather than a range of situations confronting a given observer; second, our attention is focused on the response to a given situation of decisionmakers in a particular state rather than in a number of states; and third, even if the relevant comparative material were available, methodological obstacles would still arise, since the different perspectives of separate actors—associated with a peculiar geographical position, history, expectation, national character, military strength, and national interest—might invalidate any possibility of comparison anyway. It would be unrealistic to assume, in the absence of *ceteris paribus*, that only a single variable—political system—could account for the variance of perception between different actors.

Given that these ideal investigatory conditions are neither available nor feasible, an alternative, weaker, but not totally unsatisfactory criterion remains open: to demonstrate on *a priori* grounds that the political structure of a given actor was distorting the input and assessment of information. This could be done by proving that, for instance,

(a)   a given political structure prevented conflicting evidence from reaching the decisionmaker, so that the basis of any judgment would be biased from the outset; or

(b)   that it insulated the decisionmaker from the sort of debate between conflicting assessments that might permit him to readjust an initially erroneous perception of the situation.

By comparing the salience of such effects over the range of our examples one might, with due reservations, arrive at some general hypothesis, later to be tested under more rigorous conditions.

In the 1875 case there is no indication that personality factors played a significant role in the perception of threat. No discrepancy existed on 10 April between the public response to the *Norddeutsche Allgemeine Zeitung* and *Post* articles—"great dismay" on the Paris *Bourse* was reported by the German ambassador—and the response of French decisionmakers. Within the decisionmaking group itself a common anticipation of an imminent German attack was shared by President MacMahon; the president of the council, de Broglie; and his foreign minister, Decazes. Even Thiers, the leader of the opposition in the Assembly, expressed fears of German intentions and, according to the Russian ambassador, placed his services at the disposal of the government.[2] National security was seen as taking precedence over considerations of party interest, a classic and well-known response in periods of perceived national emergency.

This very unanimity in the face of a perceived German threat is a further indication that the 1875 war scare cannot be understood purely as a narrowly defined affair of government but must be placed within the broader realm of collective phenomena. French decisionmakers cannot be considered separately from their compatriots. All shared in a common suspicion, fear, and hatred of Germany, and in a posttraumatic sensitivity to the possibility of a renewed German invasion. If one defines *public opinion* in its widest possible sense as the shared attitudes and judgments of a single national community, then the 1875 crisis should be considered an example *par excellence*, of the potent influence exercised by such opinion on the process of perception. It was not merely a question of the exercise of pressure on the government through channels shaped by the political structure, but of a collective response within which decisionmakers were spontaneous participants.

Norman Luttbeg, in his seminal essay on the link between public opinion and leadership policy, distinguishes between five different models of influence: the classic *rationalist/activist* model, which posits the direct responsiveness of representatives to the constituency that put them in power; the *political parties* model, which focuses on the function in the process of an intermediate institution, namely the political party; the *pressure groups* model, which speaks for itself; the *sharing* model, which sees representatives sharing the views of their electorate without coercion; and the *role-playing* model, which views leaders as both delegates and trustees of the public.

Of these different models it can be seen that the sharing model best corresponds to the facts in the 1875 case. There was no question of the exercise of coercion. Rather, as Luttbeg argues, a policy "abhorred by the electorate" was "equally abhorrent to the representatives, causing them to satisfy public opinion merely by action on their personal opinions." The reason for this identity of views lies in a common process of socialization and, I might add, in shared national experiences: "So long as leaders are not treated from their early childhood as a class apart, they will share life experiences with other citizens and be exposed to the same culture."[3]

In contrast to the war scare of 1875, the 1889 crisis was purely an internal government affair, news of which did not reach the general public for over a week. The first hint of any official concern appeared obliquely in the controlled press of 22 July 1889 and this, to play down the crisis with the probable purpose of signalling to France that Italy herself possessed no belligerent intentions.[4] Within the Italian government itself there was a clear difference of opinion between Crispi and Giolitti, his minister of finance, as to the authenticity of the threat. Giolitti claims to have argued that the possibility of a French invasion of Italy was quite incredible. But this solitary difference of opinion is clearly insufficient to demonstrate the peculiarity of Crispi's perception of the situation, and unfortunately, information on the reactions of other civilian members of the government is not available. No control group exists, therefore, against which Crispi's perceptions can be compared. If, however, we are prepared to turn to a less rigorous criterion of proof and evaluate Crispi's perception of threat in the light of both his previous record and the objective evidence for threat in July 1889, the importance of Crispi's personality becomes readily apparent.

All the evidence on Crispi points to an extreme sensitivity to threatening signals and an unusual degree of free-floating anxiety (one of the predispositional factors suggested by Pruitt). At a distance of so many years and without access to his medical case history, it would be going too far to diagnose him as paranoid. Nevertheless, he did display many of the characteristics usually associated with this condition. He was "characteristically suspicious and vigilant, living in a world teeming with potential dangers and implied threats."[5] Salvemini, one of his most perceptive biographers, saw him as obsessed by an "unknown monster."[6] Stillman, writing in 1889, while his subject was still alive, described him as "a conspirator by evolution if not by birth, secretive, reticent, conscious to excess of his own abilities, and contemptuous of the common ways of making them known; taciturn, moody, and indifferent to the opinion of others to an extraordinary degree."[7] To this list can be added "a tendency to suspicion, a fear of enemies and traps,"[8] and the incessant belief that he was the continued object of the hostile intentions of others. Prior to the 1889 scare he lived in the grip of the conviction, as his diaries and the Italian documents demonstrate repeatedly, that France was engaged in a concerted campaign of subversion, conspiracy, and espionage against Italy. It is true that from about 1885 to 1889 France was dominated by Boulangism, an extreme nationalist movement calling for the reconquest of the lost provinces. But Rudini, Crispi's immediate predecessor as foreign minister, was not unduly concerned by this agitation, which, at any rate, was focused on the Alsace-Lorraine issue. By the time Crispi arrived in office, the movement had passed its peak. It is no coincidence that Salisbury, Kalnoky, and Bismarck grew immune to Crispi's frequent appeals for help against a danger that never materialized. Not only was Crispi especially vigilant to danger signals; he was also uncritical of their accuracy. Giolitti emphasizes the dubiousness of the source of the information of 12 July 1889, which Crispi himself considered to be "perfectly trustworthy." Nor was his "unknown monster" subject to rational argument or disproof. At best, it remained dormant, until aroused by some further episode.

The paranoid, it is usually argued, sees others as untrustworthy, threatening, and aggressive because of a tendency to project onto them his own hostile and aggressive impulses. That Crispi was also belligerent and aggressive is again borne out by the evidence of his career—of his early revolutionary activities, of his inflammatory speeches, of his abiding hostility towards France and the papacy, and finally of his aggressive drive for imperial expansion in Africa which led to his downfall after the catastrophic Italian defeat at Adowa in 1895. In 1885 one observer doubted whether Crispi could survive in his new position as prime minister because of a tendency "to be dragged into acts and words neither fitting nor convenient to one who is chief of the government in a free state."[9] Here was one prediction proved, if belatedly, correct.

Crispi was not only aggressive and obsessed by suspicion, but also never concealed his belief in authority and the concentration of power. Arguing that a decisive foreign policy required stability and authoritarianism at home, Crispi overrode the formalities of parliamentary procedure, elevated the office of prime minister by creating a new secretariat for it, took over the ministries of Foreign Affairs and the Interior, and ruled by executive fiat.[10] He relied on his own private network of intelligence agents and at a time of crisis—such as the July 1889 scare—narrowed down the immediate decisionmaking group to include, besides himself, only the service ministers and the chief of staff, military men who could be expected to share his view of a virile foreign policy. Now this institutional structure, created by Crispi as a vehicle for his personal and undivided exercise of power, had an important influence on his perception of threat. It insulated him, first from alternative and perhaps contradictory sources of information, and second from divergent assessments of the situation. Giolitti, for instance, having dared to express his skepticism of Crispi's version of events, was permitted to play no further consultative role in the management of the crisis. In this way Crispi cut himself off from the possibility of any corrective information and reinforced an idiosyncratic and erroneous perception of the situation. He was not a victim of "groupthink", the process, described by Irving Janis, by which decisionmaking groups impose intellectual discipline on their members.[11] Crispi was an architect of groupthink.

Two conclusions can be drawn from the Crispi case: first, that a dogmatic and authoritarian personality can create a political environment which may tend to reinforce any inherent receptivity to threat (the case of Stalin in 1941 suggests itself as a counterexample); second, that this enclosed and dictatorial political environment may exist, as it did here, independently of the formal, constitutional nature of the regime. For all the use Crispi made of critical opinion, independent advisers, and his ministerial colleagues, he might well have been the head of an autocratic government, not one responsible to the electorate.

If personality factors were instrumental in 1889, there is no evidence of their salience in 1913: no sign of an exaggerated or idiosyncratic reaction on the part of Sazonov, or a discrepancy between his perceptions and those of the wider decisionmaking group. On the contrary, Russian decisionmakers were unanimous as to the threatening nature of the von Sanders appointment. Giers, the ambassador in Constantinople;[12] Neratov, the deputy foreign minister; Sazonov; Kokovtsov, the prime minister; and the czar himself[13] all expressed their dismay that a German general should be placed in command of the garrison at Constantinople. Given the sensitive nature of the issue and the historical-emotive connotations attached to the Turkish capital, any other response is difficult to imagine.

As for public opinion, it had no opportunity directly to

influence the perceptions of Russian decisionmakers in the early and formative stages of the crisis. Reports on the German mission began to appear in the Russian press only at the end of November, three weeks after the first news had reached the government in St. Petersburg. Nevertheless, this should not be taken to mean that decisionmakers' *anticipations* of public opinion were not a perceived or indirect factor in Russian considerations. On several recorded occasions Sazonov expressed his concern about the possible effects of the von Sanders appointment on public opinion. On the one hand this took the form of a rhetorical appeal to German representatives to beware of the negative impression that their policy would have on Russian public opinion "as soon as it became known."[14] On the other hand it took the form of fears described to British representatives that the mission "would give rise to violent comments in the Russian newspapers which would lead to a revival of Press polemics with Germany." This would lead to a cumulative deterioration in relations between the two countries and "make it more difficult for Germany and Turkey to give way."[15]

Partly this concern points to an anticipation that a press war would remove the affair from the more measured and calmer scope of diplomacy. More significantly, from our point of view, it demonstrates that Sazonov was highly conscious that once the Russian public became aware of the new appointment, it would inevitably perceive a clear threat to Russian interests and proof of German hostility. The foreign minister had already come under criticism before in the Duma for being "soft on Germany." Expectations of public opinion, if not the actual articulations of public opinion at the time, were a factor in Sazonov's perception of the situation. After all, the domestic environment defines the problem facing the decisionmaker no less than the external environment. Such certainty—and preoccupation—with the public response indicates an acute awareness on the part of Sazonov of the foreign policy norms and prejudices of the Russian community and an understanding that even should he wish to, he would be unable to ignore them. Both this intuitive feeling for public opinion and the unanimity of the Russian decisionmaking group on the issue bring out the minimal role played by purely personal considerations in the perception of threat and, on the contrary, the importance in this instance of community norms which public officials conformed to, but also shared.

Not only personal considerations were subsumed by this overriding collective dynamic, however. A further conclusion emerges from the above discussion: the essential irrelevance of the formal political structure of the Russian regime in a situation in which the perception of threat was basically culturally determined. Formally speaking, the Russian system of government in 1913 was autocratic: the czar had the responsibility for appointing or dismissing ministers and, among his other executive prerogatives, exclusive control over foreign policy. The Duma, though possessed of the pretensions of a constituent assembly, had few of its priviliges, except for the functions of proposing and criticizing policy and expressing public opinion. It had no means of enforcing its views in the field of foreign policy on a recalcitrant government, though it could, and did, criticize freely. But whether the Russian government was formally answerable to the elective representatives of the community or to a hereditary monarch was beside the point in the actual crisis, since the channels through which the collective views of the community were expressed were not external to the government and politically defined, but internal and socially determined, a product not of the constitution but of an underlying culture from which decisionmakers acquired their values and goals via the process of socialization and shared national experience.

The 1913 case provides a further interesting example of the working of Luttbeg's "sharing" model of public opinion—leadership linkage. Clearly, what Sazonov meant by "public opinion"—the views of a small, literate minority—is rather different from the meaning of the term in a modern Western context. It would have been inconceivable for Luttbeg's "coercive" models of linkage—the rationalist/activist, the political parties, or the pressure groups models—to function in czarist Russia. Power was simply not structured in this way. All the more noteworthy, therefore, that the noncoercive sharing model should fit the evidence. This is a point in favor of the validity of the model as such. Moreover, it suggests that the concept of public opinion, albeit in a narrower sense than is familiar, is not an empty one, even in an authoritarian regime.

In the case of Poland in March 1939, there is significant evidence of the salience of personality in the perception of threat. Beck, the Polish foreign minister, drastically lagged behind opinion at all levels in Polish society in his assessment of the situation produced by the German entry into Czechoslovakia on 15 March, arriving at his perception of threat nearly a week after the original invasion and only then as a result of what was seen to be a quite new development in Polish-German relations portended by the Lipski-Ribbentrop meeting of 21 March. Meanwhile, the army had days earlier drawn its own ominous conclusions from the German moves and begun to take operative steps to meet a possible danger; the press had been unusually unanimous in its assessment of the danger to Poland contained in the declaration of 16 March of a German protectorate over Slovakia; Noël, the French ambassador, reported "the development of anti-German feeling among Poles of all classes and backgrounds"; in Parliament observers noted a consensus among all parties of the need "to strengthen the moral and material resistance of the country" in the face of the German threat.[16] Even the president of the republic broadcast an appeal to the nation on 19 March to "be ready to make sacrifices": Poland, he declared, would not surrender its destiny "to alien protection."[17] Only in Beck's immediate circle at the Foreign Office do we fail to find open dissent from his views, and this may be merely because of limitations in our sources.

Against this rising crescendo of popular alarm, Beck's *sang-froid* struck a strangely dissonant note. How are we to account for his unusually low responsiveness to threat and the delay in his reassessment of the situation, especially in comparison to the attitudes given such forceful and wide-spread expression by the surrounding public? A number of clues present themselves in what we know of Beck's personality. At one level Beck has been described as displaying many of the characteristics of the young man who has climbed the ladder too rapidly and easily. For instance, he had an "excessive confidence in his own capacity and judgment," and this has been claimed to be the key to his character.[18] Certainly an impression of immense self-confidence was received by some of those who came into close contact with him, including Gafencu, the Rumanian foreign minister, and Noël, the French ambassador to Poland.[19] Overconfidence in his own judgment and the relationship he had built up with Nazi Germany, and an arrogant disdain for the "less expert" judgment of others, may indeed be sufficient to account for Beck's behavior in the crisis of March 1939. Such is the version given by Gafencu. Moreover, the experimental psychologist S. E. Asch, in a famous study, has demonstrated the ability of self-confident individuals to withstand group pressures to conformity.[20]

On the other hand, if we examine the evidence about Beck with a more searching eye, a very different picture begins to emerge from behind this front of self-confidence. We see a person depressed and consumptive, a heavy drinker, and a vain braggart who surrounded himself with a sycophantic atmosphere of flattery and insisted upon his personal infallibility.[21] Diana Cooper describes a dinner with him in the summer of 1938: "He repeated himself with the persistence of a cuckoo and waved his tail with peacock vanity. . . . He has told me so often that he is 'the only Colonel Beck' that I am beginning to think that he protests too much."[22] Could it be that he was doing just that? Far from being a man able to draw on deep reserves of self-confidence, he begins to appear in certain respects as an example of the depressed type who does not enjoy an inner source of self-esteem to draw upon *in extremis* and is forced, characteristically, to turn to the reassurance of others and to alcohol in order to ward off a sense of despair and personal worthlessness.[23] Is it

purely by chance that we find Beck in his account of his period in office, *Last Report*, referring on more than one occasion to what he calls the "Polish inferiority complex"
"acquired during the time when Poland was enslaved"? Poland, he believed—and this was one of the themes of his
diplomacy—had to show the world that she was "a state objectively considerable."[24] There may be an element of projection here. This would provide one explanation for the
perpetual concern with questions of prestige and form and
the sensitivity to slights, real and imagined, which run
through the pages of Beck's memoirs.

On the basis of the preceding argument it becomes possible to provide a much more convincing explanation for
Beck's low receptivity to threat and resistance to contrary
opinion in March 1939. Information about threat, just like
any other information, is assimilated to the existing cognitive
set of the individual.[25] If that information indicates that a previous decision made by the person was unwise, then it will
throw him off balance psychologically, creating what Festinger calls a state of *cognitive dissonance*. According to Festinger, we attempt to evade the discomfort associated with
this kind of imbalance by avoiding dissonant information.[26] In
the face of a clear threat, however, survival requires that we
sacrifice inappropriate policies and adjust to reality. For the
normal individual, one supposes, the price of failing to perceive threat far outweighs the discomfort of abandoning
cherished goals. But for an individual such as Beck, suffering
from an incorrigibly low sense of self-esteem, the adjustment
to reality may be far more difficult. Recognition of the German threat and a readjustment of his attitudes in March 1939
required the admission, intolerable from his point of view,
that he had been consistently mistaken in his judgment of
German intentions and that one of the very foundations of
his foreign policy—accommodation with Germany—had
been misconceived. In the short term at least, the price of
such an admission would be even higher than the failure to
perceive threat. At best he would hang on to his crumbling
policy until it became untenable. Unable to face up to the

blow to his vulnerable self-esteem contained in the original threatening information, Beck resorted to that classic mechanism for the defense of the ego—denial.

Ultimately, it became impossible for Beck to maintain his resistance to the gathering evidence of German hostility, despite its unpleasantness. Even then, Gafencu argues, Beck remained ambivalent about the German threat: "Beck perceived the danger but did not realize the catastrophe." He admitted to Gafencu in April 1939 that he had miscalculated Poland's importance for Hitler, but he still felt that the "Bolshevik danger" deterred Germany from weakening Poland, since "if the Polish bastion were to fall, the gates of Europe would be open to the Soviets' forward drive."[27]

Whether it was the weight of Polish public opinion or the accumulation of evidence that produced Beck's (albeit ambivalent) change of attitude and perception of threat is not entirely clear. Strong public pressure was brought to bear on him. There were hostile demonstrations in the streets of Warsaw, and his deputy was "badly heckled" during a foreign affairs debate in the Parliament. The latter confided to the British ambassador that "M. Beck was in an extremely difficult position. He had of course to make every effort to avoid a situation which might entail war but on the other hand he had to take into consideration the degree of feeling which had been aroused in Poland by recent events."[28] This suggests that public opinion had reached a pitch of intensity at which it necessarily became a significant component in policymaking but does not tell us what weight it in fact carried or whether it significantly altered Beck's perception of the situation.

Beck had always been able to direct Polish foreign policy with a high degree of discretion, thanks to the prestige he enjoyed as the disciple of Pilsudski in this field. He occasionally submitted a report to the president or to Smigly-Rydz, the powerful inspector-general of the armed forces, and usually gave a brief statement to the foreign affairs committee of the Sejm, or Senate, about once a year. Otherwise, he was answerable to no one.[29] In terms of the Luttbeg framework,

Beck was performing as a *trustee* rather than as a *delegate*, and thus was not directly responsive to manifestations of public opinion. Nor, unlike Decazes and Sazonov, did he share in the upsurge of popular emotion. Whatever the effect of public opinion on Beck, however, one clear conclusion can be drawn about the relationship between the structure of the Polish political system and the perceptions of decisionmakers: only in an authoritarian regime ruled by presidential decree in which the Parliament was the creature of the executive—and not the government responsible to Parliament—could a man in Beck's position, the foundations of his foreign policy having collapsed, have withstood the mounting barrage of public and parliamentary criticism without modifying his views for as long as he did. That Beck did so and still continued in office is a measure of the strength of his personal political position.

Neville Chamberlain, like Beck, had also invested heavily, in terms of effort and faith, in the possibility of cooperation with Nazi Germany. After becoming prime minister in 1937, he had persistently attempted to negotiate with Germany, especially in the colonial and economic spheres, as a prelude to a general settlement in Europe. And Chamberlain, like Beck, found it equally difficult to face up to the realization, when the Germans entered Prague in March 1939, that his hopes had been misplaced. In the British press, Parliament, and the Foreign Office the sense of disillusionment and betrayal was acute. While the *Times*, which had always strongly supported Chamberlain's policy, reacted equivocally to the invasion, the overwhelming sentiment of the national and local press was that appeasement had been totally discredited.[30] The House of Commons, Harold Nicolson noted in his diary as early as 14 March 1939, was "in a dreadful state about the partition of Czechoslovakia."[31] By 16 March this had crystallized into a general feeling that some kind of concrete action would have to be taken as a British response to the German move.

In the Cabinet on 15 March both the secretaries of state for war and for foreign affairs expressed the view that Germany had departed on a new and menacing course. Against the backdrop of this very widespread feeling of condemnation and alarm, the reaction of Chamberlain (and his closest supporters, such as Simon, the chancellor of the Exchequer, and Dawson, editor of the *Times*) was conspicuous in its quiescence. The only evaluation Chamberlain offered to the Cabinet of 15 March was that "Hitler was disappointed in not being able to stage a military triumph in the Autumn . . . the military occupation was symbolic, more than perhaps appeared on the surface."[32] In other words, things were not as bad as they appeared. In Parliament the prime minister was equally noncommittal.

At this point the substantive difference between the Polish and British forms of government becomes apparent. If Beck was not accountable to a constituent assembly, Chamberlain's position was ultimately dependent on a majority in the House of Commons. As Nicolson wrote on 17 March, "The feeling in the lobbies is that Chamberlain will either have to go or completely reverse his policy. Unless in his speech tonight he admits that he was wrong, they feel that resignation is the only alternative."[33] The political correspondent of *The Spectator* reported that the government would have to show very soon that it was fully alive to the German danger and prepared to take the most drastic steps to meet it, or face "a revolt of Government supporters."[34] Advice to this effect had already been given to Chamberlain the day before by Halifax, the man widely considered to be the natural replacement for Chamberlain as prime minister. Failure to make Britain's attitude to further German aggression plain, he argued, would lead to "insurrection both in the Conservative Party and the House of Commons."[35]

The result of this pressure was the prime minister's Birmingham speech of 17 March. His original "restrained and cautious exposition" on the Czechoslovak affair, Chamberlain explained, had been due to only "partial" information which the government had not had "time to digest." This had given "rise to a misapprehension, and some people thought that because I spoke quietly . . . I did not feel strongly on the subject." He went on to condemn, now forthrightly, the German invasion.[36] Dawson listened to the broadcast over the radio and commented in his diary: "He said all the right things about Hitler's broken pledges—rather as if speaking to a brief, as indeed he was. No doubt it put him right after his restraint in the House of Commons."[37]

All the evidence, therefore—not least Chamberlain's own revealing opening remarks—confirms that Dawson was right about the influence of political pressure on the composition of the Birmingham speech. As in Luttbeg's "political parties" model, the prime minister had been coerced by the institution which formed the basis of his political power into conforming with public opinion. It would be a mistake, however, to think that Chamberlain's expressions of concern in public on 17 March were not sincerely believed and were the mere payment of lip service to public opinion. On 19 March he wrote privately to his sister: "As soon as I had time to think I saw that it was impossible to deal with Hitler after he had thrown all his assurances to the winds."[38] It seems, therefore, that Chamberlain had internalized an enforced change of attitude. Left with no alternative but to comply with the view of his party, he maintained self-respect by convincing himself that he would have arrived at his new position regardless. The phenomenon is by no means unfamiliar to the social psychologist: opinion change manifested as overt compliance, many argue, tends to become internalized.[39]

But, as one might expect, such conversions under duress tend to be less than permanent.[40] In Chamberlain's case this was also true. Before long, Henderson had been restored to his Berlin post in the face of Foreign Office opposition. At the beginning of June 1939 Chamberlain wrote that the "dominating purpose" of what remained of his political life was "to re-establish peace and a sense of security in the world." Inevitably this led him back to the path of appeasement. As soon as time was ripe, he intended to resume negotiations with Germany. He told his sister that he wished to continue discreet contacts to persuade Germany "that she has a chance of getting fair and reasonable treatment from us and others if she will give up the idea that she can force it from us and convince us that she has given it up." To the Canadian prime minister he confided that he did not like to let any friendly gesture from Hitler pass without response. Eventually, in the first week of August 1939, in response to what were thought to be chosen words from Hitler, a fresh approach was prepared—only to be brushed aside in contempt by the Nazi leader. Other things were on his mind.[41]

One final question that remains to be answered is why precisely Chamberlain found it so difficult to recognize a German threat and then only half-heartedly. To seek an explanation in terms of his character is no simple task, for, unlike Crispi or Beck, he possessed none of those tell-tale eccentricities so suggestive of some underlying psychological quirk. It is true that he was egoistic and stubborn, but then these are hardly unusual traits in a political leader. He was also extremely dogmatic, very closed-minded in terms of the Rokeach scale, but this is not an explanation, merely a restatement of the problem. Basically, his most outstanding feature was his very normality. He possessed all those middle-class, Protestant virtues valued in English public life: an attachment to hard work, absolute integrity, self-control, optimism about human nature, and moderation. The only unusual feature he possessed was a total abhorrence of violence which went even beyond the commonly shared wish to avoid another European war: "I am myself a man of peace to the depths of my soul. Armed conflict between nations is a nightmare to me." Speaking of the First World War, he reflected on "the 7 million of young men who were cut off in their prime, the 13 million who were maimed and mutilated, the misery and the sufferings of the mothers or the fathers . . . in war there are no winners, but all are losers."[42] In the British Labour Party pacifism was a familiar ideology; but for a leader of the Conservative Party, the party of "realism" and empire, it was not.

Research carried out on responsiveness to threat has found that it is negatively correlated with pacifist characteristics (belligerence was found to be highly positively correlated).[43]

Discussing this finding, Gladstone and Taylor suggest that in the same way that aggressive personalities tend to project their hostilities onto others, peaceful personalities project their own positive, trusting qualities onto others. This suggestion certainly corresponds with Chamberlain's oft-remarked view of Hitler that "here was a man who could be trusted to keep his word."

Besides the mechanism of projection, an additional reason can be adduced for Chamberlain's resistance to threatening information: that his abhorrence of violence made it difficult for him to accept information which might presage the outbreak of violence or jeopardize his unparalleled efforts to achieve a nonviolent solution to the German problem. Recognition of the German threat would be equivalent to an acceptance that war was more than a remote possibility and that his struggle for peace had been in vain.

According to the social psychologist Daniel Katz, whether or not, and under what circumstances, attitudes change depends on the function they perform. Chamberlain's belief in the necessity of a negotiated settlement with Germany in order to avoid another war fulfilled what Katz calls a *value expressive* function; that is, it served to give expression to his central values and convictions about the human condition. Such attitudes, Katz predicts, will be undermined only by a sense of dissatisfaction with one's moral self-concept, by the realization that old attitudes have become inappropriate to main values, or because such values have ceased to be maintained.[44]

In Chamberlain's case none of these conditions held; his attitude towards Germany continued to reflect his overwhelming desire to preserve the peace. Hence, an admission that Germany could no longer be considered a partner to peaceful negotiations would be a very painful personal blow indeed. At the end of a lukewarm speech to Parliament on 15 March, the prime minister admitted this openly: "Though we may have to suffer checks and disappointments, from time to time, the object that we have in mind is of too great significance to the happiness of mankind for us lightly to give it up or set it on one side. It is natural . . . that I should bitterly regret what has now occurred. But do not let us on that account be deflected from our course."[45] Only one thing could be more painful than an admission that appeasement had failed: the loss of office and of all future prospects to contribute to "the happiness of mankind" that was so important to Chamberlain.

At this point we must leave the British prime minister. Much remains obscure and unresolved: What were the origins of Chamberlain's supremely valued wish to avoid violence? How are we to account for his personal sense of mission to save the world from another war? These questions remain tantalizingly open.

From the 1946 crisis only negative conclusions can be drawn about the effect of either personality or political factors on the perception of threat. Neither weighed heavily. Despite the extreme reaction of the Truman administration to the Soviet note, the episode aroused no especial public interest and hence no pressure. As the editorial on the subject in the *New York Times* of 14 August 1946 commented, it was largely the affair of the British and Turkish governments, as the United States had no formal commitments in the Eastern Mediterranean. Otherwise, in its analysis of the implications of the Soviet proposals, the editorial very much reflected official thinking on the issue. Thus, there was no perceptible discrepancy between public opinion and emerging government policy. Within the decisionmaking group itself there existed a large measure of unanimity, and the memorandum of 15 August 1946 which analyzed the Soviet threat was a joint effort of the State, War, and Navy departments.

Rogow, in a study of James Forrestal, secretary of the navy at this time, who later committed suicide in the Bethesda Naval Hospital, has argued that his subject's private conflicts and public attitudes were inextricably connected. His obsession with Communist subversion and conspiracy in the United States (which became increasingly frenetic towards the end), his early apprehension of Soviet intentions, and his advocacy from early 1945 onwards of a tough line towards the Soviet Union were all partly a projection of inner anxieties and insecurities.[46] It would be convenient and neat to posit a link between Forrestal's unquestionably paranoid tendencies and the administration's perception of a generalized Soviet threat associated with the first moves of the Cold War. There may be such a link, though men such as President Truman had reached their own conclusions at a very early stage. But more likely, the connection is reversed: only in a period of emergent Cold War could an individual as disturbed as Forrestal have achieved a position of such responsibility. In the crisis of August 1946 itself, there is no evidence either that Forrestal played an initiatory role or that the perceptions of others equally important, such as Truman or Acheson, radically departed from those of Forrestal himself.

Having run through each of the case studies in detail, we are now in a position to pull together the threads and form some conclusions. In three out of the six cases—Italy in 1889, Poland in 1939, and Britain in 1939—personality traits did exert a significant influence on the perception of threat, in 1889 in the direction of greater responsiveness to threatening signals, and in the two cases from 1939 in the direction of a lower responsiveness, even resistance, to threat. Only in 1889 was personality a decisive factor. This suggests that whereas a vigilant decisionmaker can perceive threat independently of surrounding opinion, decisionmakers who resist such a perception ultimately fall in with surrounding opinion.

As far as the influence of public opinion is concerned, the picture is less clear and by no means consistent. In two cases, those of 1889 and 1946, public opinion did not constitute a salient factor because public interest was minimal; these were not public crises. In two other cases, those of 1875 and 1913, public opinion was not a political factor, but was decisive in a more subtle sense: it prescribed certain standards of behavior to which decisionmakers conformed, not out of political necessity but out of cultural solidarity. This is consistent with the "sharing" model of public opinion–leadership linkage proposed by Norman Luttbeg. In contrast, in the two

cases from March 1939, public opinion, unanimous in its reaction, was an important *political* component in decisionmakers' reactions. In the British case, public opinion,
expressed through Parliament and the party system, exerted
a decisive influence on Chamberlain. In the case of Poland,
public opinion, lacking defined channels of influence, had a
more problematic effect on Beck. In the short term, he resisted its influence. Had he persisted in his initial attitude
for much longer, such opinion might have played a more decisive role, if only via its influence on the top leaders, such
as Smigly-Rydz, to whom Beck was ultimately answerable.
Thus, while the decisive political effect of public opinion
comes through in only a single example, in no case do we
find decisionmakers opposing the strongly prevailing tide of
public opinion for more than a few days.

The effect of the political structure on receptivity to threat
could not be explored comprehensively because of the limited scope of this study. Many more examples would need to
be examined to cover all the combinations possible. Nevertheless, two broad generalizations emerge: first, the system
of government defines the channels of influence open to the
public and hence can facilitate or hinder the exercise of that
influence; second, the system of government is not the primary factor regulating the flow of information and advice to
the decisionmaker on the basis of which partial or distorted
views can be reinforced or corrected.

The 1939 cases provide a good example of the interrela-
tion of political structure and public opinion. Chamberlain's
responsiveness and Beck's insensitivity to contrary views
were a function of their respective relationships with their
parliaments. When public feeling expressed itself through
nonpolitical channels, internalized in the person of the decisionmaker, as in 1875 and 1913, the nature of the political
system was necessarily secondary. Finally, the 1889 case
demonstrates that a decisionmaker with authoritarian tendencies can model the decisionmaking group in his image,
irrespective of the formal political structure, and limit the
information and advice reaching him to conform to his own

prejudices. A nonresponsible system of government may theoretically facilitate such a development, but this would seem to depend on the personality and political style of the man in control.

A final conclusion to emerge from this chapter, reflected in the above paragraphs, is that the effects of personality, public opinion, and political system on the perception of threat are inextricably interwoven: the one influences the other in a system of interaction; the one defines the scope of the other. To focus on any single factor in isolation would be to do less than analytical justice to this complexity.

Chapter 12

Appraisal: Structure

So far we have examined the circumstances, external and domestic, under which threat was perceived. From such an environmental perspective, threat appears as a more invariant phenomenon than it really is. But the perception was not simply the inevitable consequence of certain defined conditions, like phenomena in physical science. Otherwise, how could one explain why, all things being equal, threat was perceived at some given point in time rather than another? If we are to formulate a more satisfactory explanation for individual occurrences of the phenomenon, we have no alternative, I believe, but to investigate in detail the nature of the cognitive process of appraisal at the center of threat perception—the method of analysis by which the perceiver drew the conclusions he did about the significance of the events in question.

Certain questions in particular require to be answered or at least posed: To what extent does the observer arrive at his conclusion purely intuitively—like the pedestrian who automatically jumps out of the way of an approaching car—and to what extent is it the outcome of a conscious effort to reason out the significance and implications of his initial observation? Or is perhaps this distinction an arbitrary one anyway in that even the conclusions of reasoned analysis are distorted, if not determined, by prejudice, presupposition, and a degree of intuition? If the conclusion is reached intuitively, what are the grounds for this intuition? If the conclusion is the product of reasoned analysis, is the reasoning of the observer systematic? To what extent are alternative explanations for the observed phenomenon considered, or does the observer consider only a single explanation? What is the logical structure, if any, of the reasoning process?

In order to examine these sorts of questions, we must reconstruct and to some extent abstract the steps in the argument of observers in each one of our cases of threat perception. We can then decide whether these logical steps are or are not well-formed, what assumptions, implicit or explicit, lie behind them, and finally, whether or not the different arguments are linked by any common pattern of reasoning or structure.

The 1875 crisis provides an interesting initial example of the less-than-straightforward nature of threat appraisal in international relations. Here, we have the contrast between a protracted reasoning process in which Decazes struggled intellectually to make sense of a large variety of clues at his disposal, and a brief and seemingly intuitive moment of realization accompanied by signs of panic; the infusion of biased assumptions into an otherwise logical reasoning process; and finally, the way in which a fairly rational decisionmaker weighed up and hesitated between alternative explanations of the evidence before him.

By the beginning of April 1875 a large and diverse body of evidence had accumulated in the French Foreign Ministry. It included an intermittent German press campaign accusing France of rearming in order to prepare for a war of revenge, a German diplomatic *démarche* in Brussels (and, it was believed, in Rome) demanding legislation to prohibit Catholic attacks on the German government, a German Imperial Decree prohibiting the export of horses for military purposes, repeated German diplomatic protests over supposed French military preparations, the visit by a high-ranking German official to St. Petersburg allegedly to discuss with the Russian government the possibility of war with France, and intelligence reports of munitions orders and military preparations in Germany set for the end of June 1875. I have enumerated the range of evidence available to Decazes in order to emphasize the nature of his analytical problem at the time.

Strictly speaking, at least five possible explanations could have been given, or would at least have to be considered, for this body of evidence:

1. That, appearances notwithstanding, the evidence did not in fact indicate purposive intent—the prospect of some kind of German action directed against France—but was made up of a misleading juxtaposition of half-truths, exaggerations, inaccuracies, and coincidencies;
2. That Germany was engaged in a campaign of insinuation and intimidation intended to dissuade the French government, through the hinted threat of the use of force, from continuing its ongoing reorganization of the French Army;
3. That the evidence, though accurate, gave no indication of any plan or purpose but was merely the consistent and sincere expression of genuine German fears of French military preparations;
4. That Bismarck, at the height of his struggle against Ultramontane influence at home, had decided on a general anti-Catholic campaign abroad;
5. That Germany was indeed making final diplomatic, propaganda, and military preparations for an imminent attack on France.

To the credit of Decazes, most of these alternatives were considered at one time or another during the course of the crisis. Alternative 1, always the most likely explanation in the opening stages of a situation of this kind, clearly declined in credibility as evidence accumulated. Alternative 3—ironically, at least a partial explanation for the behavior of an unsettled Bismarck—was dismissed, understandably enough, by Decazes on the grounds discussed in Chapter 10: that the French Army, as the world knew, was in a position to threaten nobody, let alone Germany. Decazes's dismissal of the possibility demonstrates both a human tendency to reject the irrational and the danger of doing so. On the other hand, even though Decazes may have given insufficient consideration to this factor—as we now know, with the benefit of the hindsight provided by the German documents—this is not to say that he was being illogical. It was not unreasonable for Decazes to give a low weight to Bismarck's own imaginary fears. It is for the researcher to note that the improbable should not always be lightly dismissed and that others' fears, however irrational, may well be genuine.

In order to examine alternatives 2, 4, and 5, let us consider the 1875 crisis in two distinct prethreat and postthreat stages. From 5 March to 10 April Decazes was anxious in a generalized sense without his anxiety's having any specific reference: he was suspicious of German intentions but lacked a clear conception of how events would develop. Clearly we can account for this vague sense of foreboding in terms of his bad-faith model of Germany. Significant in this respect is Lord Lyons's remark that when he saw the French foreign minister on 15 March the latter was "in a greater state of alarm about the intentions of Germany than anything specific he told me seemed to warrant."[1] Decazes was not yet in a position to give precise definition to his fears. Intellectually he could not opt for alternatives 2 or 5 on the basis of the available evidence; intuitively he felt disturbed and alarmed. We can even detect a sort of tension between his emotive and intellectual drives. In policy terms his intellect remained paramount, however. He concluded that while there was a warning here of "impending trouble," the German moves of the previous month in Brussels and, it was believed, in Rome suggested hypothesis 4 as the most likely explanation for German behavior: Bismarck was engaged in some kind of general campaign against the Catholic Powers, within the framework of the *Kulturkampf* against Roman Catholicism, rather than one specifically directed against France. Decazes's principal policy reaction, therefore, was to request papal support in pressing moderation on the French bishops.[2]

Decazes's initial assessment that German warnings were indiscriminately directed at Catholic Europe tended to be confirmed by the Venice meeting on 2 April of the Austrian emperor and the king of Italy. News of German diplomatic and military preparations did not necessarily indicate an impending German move against France; the possibility of a German move against Italy was even mentioned. But the German press campaign, beginning on 5 April, with its accusations of French preparations for a war of revenge, made it increasingly difficult to maintain alternative 4. True, France was still classed together with Austria and Italy in the ranks of the Catholic Powers, but references to France were becoming more pointed and specific. By 10 April the official *Norddeutsche Allgemeine Zeitung*—which was known to be Bismarck's mouthpiece—while claiming to correct the impression given by the *Post* on the previous day, merely specified more clearly the charges against France and acquitted Austria and Italy of hostile intent.

At this point alternative 5, a German attack on France, looked inescapable to Decazes, to the French government, and as far as we can tell, to the public in general. Decazes expressed the fear that Bismarck would choose a "terrible lesson" for France; diplomatic observers described the "terror" of the French govenment. This sudden, general panic was sparked off by two newspaper articles! It is true that evidence had accumulated over a considerable period, but in coldly logical terms the new information of 9 and 10 April was hardly decisive. At the "moment of truth," it appears, the intuitive element in Decazes's approach predominated over the intellectual.

After the crescendo of 10 April, a calmer and more reasoned approach reestablished itself. When the expected German attack failed to transpire and it became clear that it was immediately unlikely for various technical reasons, Decazes switched to alternative 2. Germany strategy, it was concluded, was intended to confront France "with the alternative of an invasion or disarmament."[3] The vague, generalized dread of Bismarck remained, but was subsumed by more orderly processes of analysis.

What, in fact, was Decazes's method of analysis? We have seen that Decazes did his best to evaluate the relative likelihoods of the different alternatives. On the grounds for his evaluation Decazes himself provides us with a number of clues. In March he justified his anxiety by pointing out the presence of "symptoms" of "a complete program of political activity." In April he again used the expression, at a period of anxiety: "symptoms of discontent." In May, looking back over the affair, he wrote: "The frame of mind revealed by the words of Radowitz and confirmed by a set of unimpeachable symptoms could only cause profound apprehension."[4] Now a "symptom" is a phenomenon which accompanies an illness and indicates its presence. Using the method of investigation known as differential diagnosis, a physician will arrive at his analytical conclusion on the basis of a convergence of symptoms. Decazes's repeated use of the term suggests the paramount importance he attached to pattern or consistency and to the analogy between his own role and that of the diagnostic physician. Presumably he felt that while any single event might be explained away, a configuration of signals, all apparently pointing in the same direction, could be less easily dismissed. Differential diagnosis, which has reached the height of sophistication and effectiveness in modern medicine, is without doubt an impeccable and valid analytical method. Its use, however, is more problematic at the level of the state than at the level of the patient and, unless applied with caution, can be dangerously misleading. Logically speaking, one can point out that the mere existence of a pattern cannot in itself constitute indisputable proof. The relevance of a pattern of evidence is absolutely dependent on the relevance and accuracy of the component items of information considered separately. Whereas the physician has firsthand access to his evidence, and can check the accuracy of his diagnosis by further tests in the laboratory, the decisionmaker can be far less confident of his information and of the preferability of his conclusion over rejected alternatives. Furthermore, there is always the well-known danger, emphasized by Robert Jervis among others,[5] that as a pattern begins to emerge amidst a body of evidence, it tends to become self-reinforcing. Evidence that may not be strictly material or accurate derives an added, if logically spurious significance from the prior existence of the perceived pattern. One may consider this to have been one of the reasons for the war scare of 10 April 1875: the sudden recognition of a now completed pattern, the falling into place of the final piece of the jigsaw. At this point the dividing line between the logical analytical approach of differential diagnosis and the intuition of pattern (or *gestalt*) recognition becomes hazy and indistinguishable.

In the 1889 case it is difficult to discern any attempt on the part of Crispi at systematic or any other sort of reasoned analysis. There was no consideration of possible alternative explanations of the evidence, nor is there any sign that the chance of a French attack was objectively evaluated. Rather, Crispi's response was overwhelmingly intuitive and emotional. Evidence was minimal, his conclusion idiosyncratic, the role of predispositional and personality factors paramount.

In an atmosphere of gloom and an expectation of impending disaster, Crispi was faced on 12 July 1889 with two items of information, both emanating, it is noteworthy, from sources within the Vatican. The first was a certainly provocative article in the *Osservatore Romano* stating that if the pope were to leave Italy, it would be to return before long. The second was a report from an agent employed at the Vatican of an imminent French attack. At least four logical explanations could be given for this information:

1. That sources within the Vatican were attempting to use veiled threats to warn off the Italian government from anticlerical provocations and that the report of a French attack was deliberately leaked;
2. That the report of a French attack was not even contrived,

merely mistaken, for instance by an agent drawing un-warranted conclusions from the *Osservatore Romano* report;

3. That papal authorities had been encouraged by the French government to believe that they could rely on French support;

4. That there was to be an attack.

Nowhere do we find a clear statement by Crispi of his grounds for perceiving a French threat. Nevertheless, on the basis of his views before and during the crisis, we can reconstruct his implicit argument as follows:

(i) The pope plans to leave Rome;

(ii) The French government is encouraging the pope in this step;

(iii) The French government, sworn enemy of Italy, is seeking any excuse to pick a quarrel;

(iv) It supports the papacy and a restoration of its temporal powers;

(v) *Therefore* it intends to exploit the departure of the pope from Rome as a pretext to attack Italy and to restore the papacy to its temporal powers.

Items i and v were "confirmed" by information reaching Crispi. Items ii and iv were Crispi's basic assumptions about, or "images" of, France, derived from the known closeness of the French government to the Vatican. Item iii was a basic image of France long held by Crispi. Taken together, this objectively dubious structure of assumptions, images, and evidence clearly possessed a high degree of plausibility for Crispi. Without his underlying assumptions and images, his conclusion was quite far-fetched and based on the flimsiest of evidence (as, indeed, Giolitti immediately realized). Both key items of information were received on 12 July from the same source—the Vatican. There was no independent corroboration from French or other sources; there was neither evidence of French military preparations nor any explanation of why France should wish to attack Italy at that moment; reports of a papal departure were conditional rather than definite. Crispi's conclusion—his perception of threat— could not stand up to critical and objective scrutiny. Bismarck and Salisbury saw this at once. The high probability accredited by Crispi to the possibility of an attack was a product of presupposition and intuition. The available evidence, such as it was, was fitted into a framework of expectation and in no sense analyzed systematically and logically. Crispi was expecting trouble; he had long been convinced of French hostility. Following the papal consistory at the end of June, the question for Crispi was not *if* France would attack but *when*. The moment he received information of an "imminent" French attack, "he accepted the news as true without taking the trouble to sift it."[6]

Russian decisionmakers in 1913 were faced with a somewhat different problem from that of France in 1875 and of Italy in 1889. In the two latter cases it was a question of choosing between various alternative explanations of sets of ambiguous signals. In the case of Russia in 1913 the signal was an unambiguous statement of intent by the German government: a military mission was to be sent to Turkey, the head of which would be appointed commander of the garrison at Constantinople. Thus, while Decazes and Crispi were obliged to predict a *forthcoming* event, Sazonov was required to anticipate the consequences of a *known* event and to determine its significance for Russian interests.

Theoretically speaking, two alternative interpretations could be placed on the von Sanders appointment:

1. That the mission was a purely technical one, sent out in all innocence by the German government and intended to achieve no political advantages for Germany in Turkey;
2. That the mission was essentially a political act, intended to acquire for Germany a position of influence and predominance in Turkey, and that German protestations to the contrary were cynical and insincere.

The immediate Russian reaction was to ignore the mo-

dalities of the appointment and to see it not only as a threat
but also as a deliberate act of hostility towards Russia: "Placing Turkish troops in Constantinople under a German general must necessarily arouse our suspicion and apprehension."[7]
Such a reaction was surely inevitable given Russian sensitivity on the subject of Constantinople and the Straits. Any
Russian decisionmaker, one suspects, would have responded
similarily to the German stimulus, since any attempt by a
foreign power to achieve preponderance at Constantinople
was considered inimical to Russian interests. As Mandelstam
points out, sole Turkish domination of the Straits was one of
the basic and standing principles of Russian policy from the
nineteenth century onwards.[8]

It is surely significant that different Russian decisionmakers made use of quite different arguments to deprecate the
impending appointment. Neratov argued on 10 November
1913 to the German chargé d'affaires

(i) That the German mission would increase Turkey's
preparedness for war in the Dardanelles region, and
(ii) That the emplacement of guns on the Dardanelles
would be directed at Russia (presumably he meant
the free passage of Russian shipping).

Kokovtsov argued on 18 November 1913 to Bethmann-
Hollweg

(iii) That the ambassadors of the Great Powers would be
under German protection;
(iv) That Germany would be responsible for maintaining
order and security in Turkey (i.e., that she would be
able to influence internal political developments in
Turkey); and finally
(v) That he feared Turkey's uniting "with other powers"
(i.e., the incorporation of Turkey into the Triple
Alliance).

Sazonov argued on 22 November 1913 to Delcassé, the
French ambassador

(vi) That the move was an attempt by the Triple Alliance "to seize Turkey"; and

(vii) That it was part of a broad scheme of penetration into Asia Minor and the Eastern Mediterranean.

Each decisionmaker, in his own way, was drawing out the implications of the appointment: one saw it as creating a Turkish military threat and endangering Russian shipping into the Mediterranean; the second denied that it created a Turkish military threat and saw it largely in terms of German political predominance; the third saw it in more sweeping terms as part of the German drive to the east. The very diversity and inclusiveness of these views, reading into the appointment every conceivable implication, suggests that they were rationalizations of a conviction rather than the reasons for that conviction. First came the conviction that the predominance of a great power—and especially Germany—at Constantinople constituted a threat to Russia; this was basic and reflexive. Then came the attempt to explain and justify this intuition in more or less reasoned terms.

In attempting to understand Beck's perception of threat in March 1939 it is important to realize that he had anticipated the disintegration of Czechoslovakia for some time and had even considered this to be in the interest of Poland. Slovakia, he believed, detached from Bohemia and Moravia, would become a natural area of Polish domination, and Poland would be able to draw closer to Hungary and Rumania in the creation of a "Third Europe" between Germany and the Soviet Union and independent of both. Germany, Beck was convinced, would look with benevolence on Polish ambitions in its special area of interest, just as it had at the time of Munich. Thus, even though Czechoslovakia commanded Poland's southern approaches, Beck avoided ties of friendship with it and was not disturbed by Germany's campaign against that country. Poland was too important to Germany as a potential partner against the Soviet Union, Beck believed, for her friendship to be endangered. This conception of Beck's was made up partly of wishful thinking, perhaps, but mostly of two dominant images—of Nazi anti-Bolshevism and hence of an identity of interests, at least in this respect, between Germany and Poland; and of Poland's desirability, because of her military strength, as an ally.

With the German entry into Prague on 15 March 1939, Beck's policy and conception were thrown off balance but not quite overturned. On the one hand, Bohemia and Moravia had, as expected, fallen under German control. This made hardly any strategic difference, since it merely filled in the area surrounded by Austria in the south and Germany proper to the north and east. Furthermore, Hungary's occupation of Subcarpathian Ruthenia was welcomed as a step towards the "Third Europe," in that it created a common boundary between Poland and Hungary. On the other hand, an unexpected and unwelcome development was the announcement of a German protectorate over Slovakia without so much as consultation on the matter between Germany and Poland. From a strategic point of view alone (not paramount with Beck) this created a potential military threat recognized at once as such by the Polish Army.

How were the overall political situation and especially future German objectives to be viewed at this point? Basically, five alternative interpretations could be placed on the German occupation of Czechoslovakia:

1. That it was an end in itself and there would be no further German moves;
2. That it was part of a strategy to dominate, militarily or politically, Southeastern Europe, especially Rumania;
3. That it was part of a strategy of encirclement aimed at the military or political domination of Poland;
4. That it was a preparatory move in a strategy directed against the Ukraine and the Soviet Union;
5. That it was a combination of some, or all, of these previous possibilities.

Polish decisionmakers certainly weighed several alternative interpretations of the German move rather than merely opting intuitively and unquestioningly for a single explanation. On the basis of what we know from British documents, at least possibilities 2, 3, and 4 were considered more or less systematically. At first, Beck, still convinced of German friendship, could not believe that the occupation of Czechoslovakia was directed against Poland. On 17 March 1939 he expressed the hope "that a protectorate might not be established over Slovakia to the same degree as over Bohemia and Moravia."[9] In other words, he clung to the hope that Poland would, despite everything, be able to extend its own influence over Slovakia. The following day he rejected the possibility of a German ultimatum to Rumania (alternative 2), which would have been almost as unwelcome from the Polish point of view as a direct threat (alternative 3). He cited as evidence assurances recently received in Berlin. On 20 March his deputy minister, Arciszewski, speaking, we assume, either in Beck's name or in conformity with his views, opted for alternative 4: A "Russian or Ukraine adventure was more probable" than designs on Poland. At the same time Arciszewski differed from Beck in that he did not rule out the possibility of Germany's applying pressure to secure economic hegemony over Rumania.[10]

Until now Beck, notwithstanding his attachment to certain dominant images, had approached the problem posed by the German move rationally. There were grounds for suspicion that the move might be directed against Poland, but there was no definitive evidence one way or the other. Without the benefit of hindsight Beck could not be certain of the validity of one hypothetical explanation of the German move rather than another. His "error," if one can use such a term, was to underestimate the chance that the German strategy was, if only in part, directed against Poland; this was the product of preconception.

Any uncertainty was removed, both logically and psychologically, on 21 March 1939 by Lipski's meeting with Ribbentrop, who repeated German proposals for a renegotiation of the status of Danzig. In a tone reminiscent of previous German proposals to others, Ribbentrop advised Lipski that "the talk should not be delayed, lest the Chancellor come to the conclusion that Poland was rejecting all his offers."[11] At this point hypothesis 3 presented itself irresistably. Beck concluded at once that the German proposal was the prelude to an ultimatum; Danzig was merely a lever to be used by Germany to subjugate Poland. Here was an unambiguous perception of threat.

How logical was Beck's conclusion? There existed two possible explanations of German proposals:

(*a*) That Danzig was an isolated problem over which a compromise could be reached without wider repercussions; or

(*b*) That Danzig was a means to achieve political or military domination over Poland.

Theoretically, Danzig might have been considered an isolated problem standing in the way of Polish-German partnership. This, indeed, was the impression which the German government attempted to convey. Poland, however, had always insisted that German acceptance of the *status quo* in Danzig was a nonnegotiable condition of Polish-German cooperation. Until October 1938 the German government had accepted this condition without question. It could not, therefore, now pretend that it was unaware of the immense significance Danzig possessed for Poland. In fact, the Polish commitment to the existing status of Danzig was too firm to permit retreat. Regardless of any other consequences, surrender on this issue would deliver a damaging blow to Polish prestige and make it difficult to oppose further German demands. Beck was thus surely justified in opting for alternative *b*—that the German proposals "might only represent [the] forerunner of further demands and an eventual ultimatum."[12] Whether or not the *démarche* was intended to subjugate Poland, this would have been the consequence of its acceptance.

For the British government in March 1939 the analytical problem resolved itself into a choice between two alternative explanations of German action:

1. That the dismemberment of Czechoslovakia was an end in itself; or
2. That the action in Czechoslovakia was a prelude to a further extension of German domination.

As long as the former hypothesis could be maintained, British decisionmakers might express moral disapproval but need not conclude that British interests were threatened. Only the second alternative (or "family" of alternatives) might lead to the conclusion that British interests were threatened, and even then such a conclusion was only a possibility and not a necessity. It might still be maintained, as Halifax had argued in November 1938, that German expansion was "a normal and natural thing."

Obliged by circumstances to rethink the basic assumptions underlying British policy, British decisionmakers arrived at the realization of a German threat not suddenly, but rather, after a reappraisal stretching over two or three days. For this reason the British case is an interesting example of a chain of reasoned analysis preceding the perception of threat. At the same time it is important to recognize the ethical and cultural assumptions that underlay the analysis, and the irrational premise on which the final step in the argument was based.

Halifax's first reaction to the German move of which we have any record came at the Cabinet meeting on the morning of 15 March 1939. Understandably, the foreign secretary contented himself at this early stage with the most urgent, surface aspects of the question: a description of what had happened, a discussion of the immediate problems arising, and (most interesting from our point of view) his own personal reaction to the occupation. Halifax presented a series of propositions, grounded in certain ethical assumptions, explaining why the German move was wrong and deplorable and an infringement of good faith with Britain:

(i. *a*) That Germany had, for the first time, incorporated a non-German population.

The thrust of this allegation makes sense only in the light of the British assumption that Germany was justified in demanding the incorporation of German-speaking populations into the Reich, but equally, must respect the right of self-determination of others.

(*b*) That Germany's action was inconsistent with her commitments under the Munich Agreement.

The assumption underlying this allegation was the principle of *pacta sunt servanda*, the ethical duty of a state to maintain its obligations.

(*c*) That Germany had used force rather than peaceful negotiation.

British ministers had always insisted that, whatever German objectives, the main thing was that they be achieved by mutual agreement, peacefully arrived at. Chamberlain had made great play of Germany's acceptance of this principle in the Munich Agreement. This emphasis on methods even more than on objectives rested partly on a cultural norm, partly an abhorrence of war.

As yet, there was no attempt to work out the future implications of the German action nor its significance for British interests. On the afternoon of 15 March 1939 Halifax, having expressed his initial moral reaction, took his analysis much further in an interview with the German ambassador. His point of departure was i. *b*, that, "what had taken place was in flat contradiction with the spirit of the Munich Agreement."[13] From here Halifax made the important transition to the comments

(ii) That "nobody felt the assurances of the German government to be worth very much . . . "

This involved a generalization from the particular observation contained in i. *b*. Strictly speaking, the fact that one promise had been broken did not necessarily mean that future promises would be broken. Nevertheless, if one considers promises and other kinds of moral propositions to be based on absolute or categorical imperatives, then a single infringement or counterexample is sufficient to demonstrate that the actor in question does not keep his promises. Moreover, Halifax was careful to use the words "nobody felt." Even assuming a less rigorous approach to moral statements, it is clear that at the very least the subjective probability of Hitler's keeping future promises had fallen.

(iii) " . . . and that everybody asked themselves in what direction the next adventures would be framed."[14]

Again, strictly speaking, the transition from proposition ii to proposition iii is a non sequitur. That the German government had broken its assurances concerning Czechoslovakia need not logically entail that it would then set out on a program of further aggression. In international politics, however, where most decisions are made under conditions of uncertainty, subjective probability is the guiding light. The British government would be bound to consider the eventuality of "further adventures" more seriously, without being able to assign to the event any hard and fast estimate of probability. Hence Halifax's sensible formultion that "everybody asked themselves" rather than any more definitive phrasing.

Thus, by the afternoon of 15 March Halifax had taken the argument an important step forward: he reasoned that on the evidence of German behavior there had been a notable increase in the subjective probability that the German government would undertake further adventures. As yet, he had still not reached any specific conclusions about how this would affect the position of Great Britain. This further and final step was made explicit on 17 March in Halifax's conversation with the ambassador of the United States. In the context of a general discussion of policy alternatives the British foreign secretary now made clear

(iv) That his estimate of "the probabilities or otherwise of his own country being the object of direct attack" had changed as a result of recent events.[15]

Thus Halifax, having moved from the particular observation that the Munich Agreement had been infringed, to the general proposition that German assurances were unreliable and that further adventures might be expected, now arrived at the particular conclusion that policymaking would have to be based upon the higher probability of an attack upon Britain. It was this logical progression that underlay his appraisal of threat and the change in policy consequent upon it. The remarkable aspect of the final step in Halifax's argument—and the point at which intuitive assumptions can be seen to bias his reasoning—is that from a technical point of view Germany did not possess the means, as I have pointed out in Chapter 10, to carry out such an attack. It is true that precisely such an attack was launched upon Britain in the summer of 1940. But this came only after the catastrophic and absolutely unforeseen collapse of France. Such an eventuality was hardly taken into consideration in March 1939.

Implicit in Halifax's argument was not the scenario of a French collapse but the conviction, universally and unquestioningly held by British decisionmakers and military experts, that a breakdown in Anglo-German relations would almost inevitably be followed by a massive, sustained, and ruinous air offensive on British cities. Hence British surprise during the period of "phony war" that such an offensive was not immediately forthcoming. Clearly, air attacks on Britain were an important, indeed vital contingency to plan for in the event of a second European war. But it was surely illogical for Halifax in March 1939 to present this as a major possibility in the aftermath of the German entry into Prague. The important weight Halifax gave to this possibility in his policy considerations is only explicable in terms of the British obsession with the weakness of their air defenses and the nightmare of aerial bombing.

Our final example, the U.S. response to Soviet proposals for a revision of the Montreux Convention, like the British appraisal of March 1939, is an instance of protracted analysis as the result of which threat was appraised. Two detailed memoranda, one of 15 August 1946 presented jointly by the departments of State, War, and the Navy, and one drawn up by the Chiefs of Staff on 23 August 1946, enable us to reconstruct the logic which underlay the American perception of threat.[16]

The first step in the American chain of argument (though not in the sequence of presentation) was the view

(i)   That Soviet proposals for joint Soviet-Turkish organization of defense of the Straits were equivalent to a request for military base rights at the Dardanelles and the introduction of Soviet troops into Turkey.

It is clear that the proposal to "organize joint means of defense of the Straits" does imply the introduction, at some time, of Soviet personnel into the area, either in the form of a permanent presence or of a contingency force to be moved in time of need. In any event, the second eventuality might not be very different from the first, since a contingency force presupposes the existence in the area of skeleton facilities and personnel. At the same time, this distinction is really only an academic one in the light of previous Soviet proposals to Turkey that were more explicit on this point. For example, in a note of June 1945 the Soviet government proposed to Turkey a revision of the Montreaux Convention that would include Soviet occupation of bases and possible joint control of the Straits in wartime.[17]

On the basis of item i it was then argued

(ii) That the Soviet Union would "use these forces in order to obtain control over Turkey."

There are two implicit links between steps i and ii. First there is the assumption expressed by Acheson at one of the early meetings to formulate the memorandum of 15 August 1946, that *according to the plain pattern of Russian behavior*, a Russian beachhead at the Straits would lead to Turkey's loss of sovereignty. Presumably by this he was drawing a parallel with the consequences of the entry of the Red Army into the states of Eastern Europe. This assumption demonstrates the way in which a particular event was interpreted in the light of a previously observed behavior pattern. Second, there is the linking argument, found in the memorandum of 23 August, that the Straits could not be effectively defended unless the Soviet Union extended its military base rights "to include military dominance of the area for several hundred miles in all directions." Moreover, it was argued, even nominal Soviet privileges and forces could be reinforced "in days or hours" and a bridgehead created. This would involve the "immediate military dominance of Turkey" and reduce her "to a satellite Soviet state." In other words, even if the Russian proposals were essentially defensive in intent, their acceptance would still—as in the 1913 case of the Liman von Sanders mission—enable the Soviet Union to consolidate its position at will. Soviet possession of the option was seen to be as dangerous as its actual immediate implementation.

Up to this point the American argument remains on fairly firm logical ground and can be considered well-formed. Henceforth, as American decisionmakers attempted to assess the sweeping geostrategic implications of the Soviet proposals, the argument becomes more controversial and more obviously a question of assumption, opinion, and judgment. Given that it was reasonable to conclude that in one way or another "joint defense" of the Straits would result in Soviet domination of Turkey, two alternative projections could be made of the consequences of such an eventuality:

1. That the Soviet Union, having secured its southern flank in the Black Sea area, would be content to rest on its laurels; i.e., that its objectives were basically defensive; or
2. That domination of Turkey would be used as a springboard for further expansion; i.e, that Soviet objectives were offensive.

Here was a question that had deeply troubled Americans for many months. It was impossible to be certain either way, but the second alternative, persuasively set out in the famous Kennan and later Clifford memoranda, had come to be widely accepted and was to underlay many perceptions of Soviet behavior in the Cold War period, including the one under discussion here. Hence the neglect of alternative 1. Despite this neglect—and this is the significant point as far as we are concerned—the structure of the American appraisal in August 1946 remained logical rather than intuitive; the final conclusion was arrived at on the basis of reasoned argument, and awareness, if rejection, of the alternative possibilities.

From the proposition that Soviet participation in the defense of the Straits would entail the loss of Turkish independence it was in turn agreed

(iii.*a*) That "Greece and the whole Near and Middle East, including the Eastern Mediterranean" would fall under Soviet control.

Between steps ii and iii we can detect three links: (1) The argument to capability: Soviet control over Turkey would make it "extremely difficult, if not impossible, to prevent the Soviet Union from obtaining control over Greece and over the whole Near and Middle East." (2) To be taken together with argument 1 in classic textbook fashion, the argument to intention: The Soviet Union was a dynamic, expanding power determined to extend its predominance wherever and whenever the opportunity arose. Hence, the crucial assumption at this stage of the argument was the "immutable law" of Soviet expansion. Finally (3) the exclusively military argument used by the Joint Chiefs of Staff that "the same logic which would justify Soviet participation in the defense of the Dardanelles would also tend to justify further Soviet penetration through the Aegean."

It was also agreed

(iii.*b*) That "it is our experience that when the Soviet Union obtains predominance in an area, American and, in fact, all Western influences and contacts are gradually eliminated from that area."

This is again an appeal to a "general principle" of Soviet behavior. Soviet dominance was tantamount to the exclusion of all Western influence. Alternative possibilities of, for instance, shared influence were seen to be ruled out by past (and, indeed, ongoing) experience in Eastern and Southeastern Europe and especially Germany.

At the final stage of discussion and analysis the significance of the above propositions for U.S. interests was evaluated and the following conclusions reached:

(iv.*a*) That the Soviet Union would have "full mastery" of a territory "which is strategically important from the point of view of resources, including oil and from the point of view of communications";

(*b*) That the Soviet Union would "be in a much stronger position to obtain its objectives in India and China";

(*c*) That whether or not Turkey would withstand Soviet pressure constituted a test case for the United Nations (implicitly, failure in this instance would materially weaken an organization to which the United States was deeply committed).

These are arguments found in the more general analysis of 15 August but not in the more military-oriented analysis of 23 August. To these points the latter added a further conclusion:

(*d*) That Soviet success in Turkey would gravely affect "the faith and political reliance"—that is, the credibility—of the "major non-Soviet powers" in the eyes "of the Middle Eastern peoples and nations on the periphery of the 'iron curtain.'"

Propositions *c* and *d* are similar in that they both look at Turkey as a test case for further anticipated confrontations between the United States and the Soviet Union.

Thus, we have the final step in the American argument, one largely involving value judgments of the utility or disutility of the Soviet proposals. On the basis of these value judgments it was concluded that the Soviet proposals of 7 August 1946 constituted a threat to the interests of the United States. Hence the recommendation that Turkey be supported "firmly and with determination" by the United States, "if necessary . . . with force of arms." This policy the president was prepared to pursue "to the end."

The case studies examined above possess too many individual features to permit the derivation, at this stage, of a single paradigm of threat appraisal. At best we can sketch out the range of possibilities which set the limits on the phenomenon. While we can identify the boundaries of the map, we can give no precise map reference.

An initial conclusion is that it would be misleading to label the process of threat appraisal as either reasoned or intuitive. Even when the decisionmaker thinks out a problem reasonably systematically, weighing the evidence for or against a particular interpretation, his final preference is ultimately the result of a subjective recognition or insight. No logical formula can infallibly select the most likely explanation for his observation nor set a precise probability on the occurrence of a future unique event. In the final analysis, whatever the preamble and however comprehensive the range of alternatives considered, the choice of explanation is inevitably subjective. Furthermore, no evidence can be examined in a vacuum. Evidence can only make sense against a background of beliefs and assumptions about the world. And the moment such learned experience is drawn upon, as it must, then subjective factors enter into judgment. There can be no doubt, in every one of the cases examined, of the important role played by predispositional factors in the cognitive process of threat appraisal. Whether bad faith between two countries, an obsession with a particular kind of vulnerability, or a preeminent sensitivity to developments at a particular location, such factors played a significant part in weighing the balance on the side of a particular alternative. True, in 1889 the bias was so marked as to rule out alternative interpretations of the evidence from the outset, whereas the British obsession in 1939 with air vulnerability more subtly influenced the judgment of the possibility of a German attack; nevertheless, the principle remains the same.

The cognitive process varied markedly in complexity. This

can be illustrated schematically. Let us imagine the complexity of an argument as a graph, one axis of which represents the ability of the decisionmaker to envisage a range of alternative explanations, the other his ability to follow through the consequences of those different possibilities. One coordinate measures the breadth of his reasoning, the other its depth. Put in this way we can locate the 1889 case almost in the bottom left-hand corner of the graph. Crispi showed a singleminded inability either to look beyond his one obsessive scenario of a French naval attack or to look very deeply into its consequences. High up the consequences axis, but not very far along the alternatives axis, come the 1913 and 1946 cases. In both cases we find a very detailed elaboration of one particular and unpleasant scenario, together with the complete suppression of any other alternatives. Similarly the British appraisal, at least in its prethreat stage, concentrated on detailing the consequences for Britain of the German entry into Prague. Consideration of the various alternatives did play a part in the later formulation of policy but not in the initial perception of threat. At the other extreme can be located the case of Poland in 1939 and that of France in 1875. Both can be placed rather low on the consequences axis but far along the alternatives axis. Decisionmakers in these two examples did demonstrate awareness of alternative possibilities, but followed up their consequences more narrowly.

One feature shared by all our examples is that while the range of alternatives envisaged varies considerably, never more than a single scenario, the one pregnant with danger, was elaborated in detail. Threat perception, this suggests, is associated with the inability of the observer to look beyond one particular, obsessive image of disaster. A willingness to visualize other sets of consequences would have lowered the credibility of the unquestioned scenario. Why the observer was preoccupied with one single image is answered by the earlier chapters on predispositional factors. Certain dangers are selected by experience as especial objects of concern, and even before any crisis develops these dangers have been imaginatively rehearsed and planned for. They are expected.

When the crisis does occur, signals are interpreted in the light of anticipations and images of disaster dominate decisionmakers' thoughts. Other possibilities are neglected.

A final perspective from which to compare and contrast the results of this chapter is provided by John Steinbruner's stimulating and innovative analysis of decisionmaking theory.[18] Steinbruner distinguishes between three explanatory models of decisionmaking (equally applicable to problem-solving in general): the analytic paradigm, the cybernetic paradigm, and the cognitive paradigm. In the *analytic paradigm* the decisionmaker places values in order of preference, evaluates alternative outcomes in terms of their relative probabilities, and is reasonably open to new information about central aspects of a problem. Unfortunately, Steinbruner argues, this classic, rational model of decisionmaking tends to be discredited by famous historical blunders, such as the Japanese decision to attack the United States in 1941. In the *cybernetic paradigm* the decisionmaker neither evaluates alternative outcomes nor considers information relevant to the manifold aspects of a problem. To protect himself against overwhelming complexity, he is sensitive only to information entering through certain established channels relevant to a few predetermined factors, he processes that information according to certain standard operating procedures, and he implements his response from among a limited repertoire on the basis of certain simple principles. Animal communities and bureaucratic organizations provide examples of this mode of decisionmaking. Finally, *cognitive theories* of decisionmaking, closely associated with experimental psychology, stress our defective and biased, if earnest attempts at understanding. Decisionmakers are seen as tending to conceptualize problems in terms of a single value, associate only a single outcome with available alternatives, and restrict information utilized to a relatively narrow band of variables. Steinbruner himself considers a combination of the cognitive and cybernetic paradigms to give the best empirical description of decisionmaking in international politics.

The case studies here cast doubt on the rather too clear-cut distinctions posited by Steinbruner's analysis. All three paradigms could be roughly applied, separately or in combination, to one or another of our examples: the analytic model partly corresponds to the process of judgment displayed by Decazes and Beck; the cybernetic model corresponds quite accurately to the appraisals of Russian decisionmakers in 1913, of the Polish high command in March 1939, and of the Joint Chiefs of Staff in 1946; the cognitive approach covers aspects of most of the cases. On the whole, though, one would prefer to avoid characterizing the process of threat appraisal in terms of any single paradigm or synthesis of paradigms. If there is a common pattern linking our different examples of cognitive judgment, it is not to be found in the formal structure or style of the analysis used.

In the following chapter, however, I shall suggest that at a decisive link in the chain of argument, lying at the core of threat appraisal, there is indeed a common theme. And this may provide us with a key to the overall phenomenon.

Chapter 13

Appraisal: Theme

According to the distinguished logician Susan Stebbing, "a distinguishing characteristic of intelligence is the ability to discern relevant connexions—to put together what ought to be conjoined and to keep distinct what ought to be separate." At the basis of reasoned thought is the process of deriving well-formed conclusions from given statements whose truth is already established. Provided that we know that one statement entails another, and also that the former is true, then we can validly infer that the latter is true. In this way we can sometimes obtain new knowledge—make use of knowledge we already possess in order to discover something we did not know.[1]

To the extent that problem-solving in international politics is based on an attempt at reasoned thought, the decisionmaker is placed in the identical position of any other thinking individual, though since he can never be certain that the premises of his argument are necessarily true, even an impeccably well-formed argument may still generate untrue conclusions. But putting this reservation to one side we can see that the decisionmaker, like any other intelligent being, is required to draw correct (and, of course, relevant) conclusions on the basis of certain statements—items of evidence—about the physical environment. When it comes to the perception of threat, necessary if the decisionmaker is to fulfill his vital duty of protecting the interests of the state, at the core of which lie national integrity and independence, he must also "put together what ought to be conjoined." Namely, the decisionmaker evaluates whether or not certain statements about the behavior of another actor, which have been received from various sources of information, are sufficient grounds for the conclusion that the opponent is engaged in, or intends to engage in, a course of action damaging to the perceiver.

Unfortunately, as any observer of the international scene knows only too well, it is rarely that the decisionmaker comes into possession of evidence of a syllogistic kind sufficiently adequate or reliable to enable him to draw certain conclusions. In other words, the perception of threat is invariably based on a deductive step—a leap in the dark—that necessarily goes beyond the limited information inherent in the original evidence. No logical causeway can guide the steps of the observer from the ambiguous pattern of information at his disposal to the firm ground of the safe deduction. Only a ramshackle rope-bridge extends across the chasm of uncertainty.

In other cases of perception, but not of threat perception in international politics, the logical progression from premises to conclusion is often aided by past induction: the learned experience that all previous cases of a given cue have indeed been evidence of the existence of a particular phenomenon. As we have already noted, however, threat perception is rarely a case of object recognition. Indeed, in the six examples we have studied there is no case of this kind.

The crucial question, therefore, is, What is the logical basis of the deduction in threat appraisal from premise to conclusion, given that it is neither a logical necessity nor determined by previous inductive inference (i.e., learned experience)?

The answer to this question will take us a long way toward understanding the logic of threat perception. We have already established, in the previous chapter, that no single logical structure characterized the six different cases of threat perception in international crisis. Let us, accordingly, try to isolate the decisive transition, from the point of view of its thematic content, between evidence and threatening conclusion in each of our case studies.

The crucial inference, central to the appraisal of threat, is found in the recurrent argument that the opponent had in some way betrayed a trust or undertaken an illegitimate and unpermissible action—that he had somehow infringed a norm of behavior—and that, *as a consequence of this*, he had ceased to be bound by existing restraints and was to be considered as bent on a policy of aggressive domination gravely damaging to the interests of the observing actor. Having perceived that the opponent had thrown over one set of normative restrictions, the evidence for which consisted in the observer's original information on the opponent's conduct, the observer was forced to conclude that the opponent was no longer playing the "game" according to the "rules" and had rejected those conventional and limited objectives of the diplomatic "game" for something far more sinister and unpredictable.

In the war scare of 1875 the accumulation of evidence indicated, to French decisionmakers, not simply that Germany was about to attack. In reality, this was merely the form taken by the danger at one point in the crisis. The issue in French eyes was more profound. It was whether France, despite defeat and occupation, was to be permitted to exercise the prerogatives of a sovereign state. Germany, French observers believed, had as a primary objective the denial of what was seen to be the most fundamental of state rights, that "of every nation to constitute and to dispose of her military forces at her own will."[2] German threats, hints, complaints, and recriminations on the subject of French rearmament confronted the French government with an impossible choice: in Decazes's agonizing words " the alternative of an invasion or disarmament." In either case France faced the appalling prospect of ceasing to function as a sovereign and independent state. The German campaign, therefore, was seen to constitute an attack on one of the very normative pillars of the international system.

Once German conduct in 1875 departed from a norm as fundamental as the noninterference of one state in the sovereign affairs of another, the entire structure of European politics was perceived to be endangered. Decazes, writing on 10 April 1875 at the very height of the crisis, described German accusations in the *Post* and *Norddeutsche Allgemeine Zeitung* as "the prelude to an action of which I cannot foresee all the bearings." And then, with significant overstatement and sense of horror: France was to be chosen for "the terrible lesson through which [Bismarck] intends to cure Europe of her relative independence." The Old World was to be "mastered and laid under the yoke of German terror [*furor teutonicus*]."[3] Having forsaken the rules of the existing diplomatic game, Germany appeared to be bent on a new and unpredictable course which might be directed not only at renewing the occupation of French territory, but also at toppling the very balance of power in Europe. Those writers who analyze the crisis in terms of Decazes's cleverly exploiting a series of trumped-up rumors fall wide of the mark.[4] They fail to grasp the importance of international norms of behavior and the far-reaching implications of infringements of legitimacy. As Decazes saw it, German conduct gave evidence "of a mental attitude not only hostile to France, but fiercely opposed to its national existence." These words were written on 29 April 1875, when he was aware that there was no "immediate and direct danger."[5] They can be read as an indication of the dismay felt by Decazes at a state of affairs in which France was not to be permitted to pursue an independent, sovereign policy. It was to put an end to this, not to win some narrow and momentary gain, that he mobilized the support of the Russian and British governments.

There are a number of important similarities between the 1875 and 1889 cases. In both instances the perception of threat took the form of a fear of invasion while developing out of a crisis in which the observer saw the sovereignty and legitimacy of the state questioned and infringed by the opponent. In 1889 the point of departure of the affair was a secret consistory held at the Vatican on 30 June 1889. Now at this time, the status of the papacy rested on the Guarantee Law of 13 May 1871, which restricted the sovereignty of the pope to the area of the Vatican and deprived him of his former surrounding territories. Hereby—and this is the operative point—the incorporation of Rome and the Papal States into the Kingdom of Italy was formally legitimized. Thus, the settlement constituted one of the foundation stones of the Italian state. Any attempt to call this settlement into question would at one and the same time cast doubt on the very legitimacy of the new Italy. And this was precisely the position taken by the Vatican, with some support from French circles. From the first the Vatican refused to recognize the settlement and, most menacingly from the point of view of Italian nationalists (and Crispi was more sensitive than most), did not hesitate to call for the help of other Catholic countries in the overthrow of Italy and papal repossession of its lost territories. Persistence in this attitude, and support for it by French clericals, among others, continued to be one of the most potentially serious and unresolved problems facing Italian governments. Here we come back to 1889 and the invasion scare. Whatever the truth of the matter, Crispi firmly believed, and constantly reiterated, that at the secret consistory of 30 June the departure of the pope from Rome had been agreed upon. At one stroke this would signal the termination of the vital, if uneasy, existing arrangement between Italy and the Vatican. Such an abrogation of the *status quo* would withdraw one of the linchpins from the Italian state and jeopardize the very structure of Italian unity.

Providing one grasps the importance of the status of the Vatican and of Rome as established in 1870–71 in Crispi's conception of the normative foundations underlying Italy's place in the international community, it becomes much easier to explain the nature of his fears (though not, perhaps, his acute sensitivity and imperviousness to counterargument).

Like Decazes, Crispi perceived that any aspersion or damage to national sovereignty and legitimacy bore with it a threat to national existence itself. He hardly dared "to face the consequences of a conflict whose results no one can foresee."[6] French support for papal claims was seen as the tip of an immense iceberg of subversion and aggression directed against Italy. At first Crispi feared a French attack on land and sea; then a coordinated Russo-French attack on the Triple Alliance; and finally, the French use of revolutionary agents to turn Italy against Austria and, "in the event of war breaking out between Italy and France, to foment the breaking out of a revolution against the Monarchical system."[7] In the same conversation Crispi jumbled together, in a comprehensive and indiscriminate kaleidescope of menace, images of external attack, internal subversion, and embracing conspiracy. By seemingly infringing the "rules," France was perceived to endanger the very unity and continued viability of the Italian state.

In the Russian view the von Sanders appointment of October 1913 infringed the "gentleman's agreement" governing conduct between the powers at Constantinople. When Sazonov first learned of the mission in May 1913, he had attached no particular importance to it because he understood it to fall within the scope of previous German missions to Turkey and hence to conform to a stable and acceptable pattern of conduct. The mission appeared in quite a different light once it turned out that, unlike his predecessors, von Sanders was to exercise personal command at Constantinople. This point was strongly emphasized in the Russian draft note of 7 December 1913. Von Sanders, it was argued, would be in a position "which hitherto neither a German nor any other officer has ever occupied in Constantinople. . . . The actual guarantee of the integrity of the Turkish Empire, which consists in the balance of powers, would have vanished."[8]

Russian decisionmakers were in fact referring to a very specific agreement to maintain the *status quo* on which the "balance of powers" was based which had been arrived at verbally between the Great Powers at one of the sessions of the Ambassadors' Conference, held in London on 18 December 1912, to discuss a settlement of the First Balkan War. At this meeting the French ambassador had read out a proposal, at the instructions of his government, that "as far as Constantinople is concerned we are firmly attached to the maintenance of the *status quo*. The city should, therefore, remain in the possession of the Ottoman Empire." No one raised any question or objection on this; and according to all accounts of the meeting, including the German and the Russian, the proposal was adopted unanimously.[9]

Agreement to the *status quo* at Constantinople was part of a wider censensus between the Great Powers, reflected in their discussions on the subject during the period of the Balkan Wars of 1912–13, that as long as the Ottoman Empire remained intact it was best to leave the existing situation undisturbed. Only in the event of the collapse of the empire, when partition would become unavoidable, need the nettle be grasped. Even at the height of the Liman von Sanders crisis, the Great Powers continued to affirm the need to maintain the integrity of Turkey.[10]

Russian decisionmakers had an additional reason for their sense of grievance at the German appointment. This was the German failure to consult with the Russian government on the impending mission and its extended functions—an issue which patently affected Russian strategic and sentimental interests in the area. Sazonov and his colleagues repeatedly expressed their surprise and resentment at what they considered to be a betrayal of trust. Sazonov in particular found it extraordinary "that this serious question was not touched upon by the chancellor [Bethmann-Hollweg] at the time of my frank and friendly conversations with him" of the previous month.[11] Having engaged in these talks in order to create a better climate of understanding between the two states in the Near East, the Russian foreign minister now discovered that a vital area of concern had been withheld from his attention. Then, when the Russian ambassador in Constantinople had actually inquired about the mission, he had been misled as to its scope. Even when a more complete picture of the nature of the mission had emerged, the German government had continued to be less than open in its exchanges with the Russians. Significantly, Sazonov attempted to appeal to Russo-German "friendship" in his meeting of 17 November 1913 with the German chargé d'affaires and returned to the theme of German "promises" on 22 November. He clearly felt that he possessed grounds for complaint in the matter.

As a result of his perception that Germany had over-stepped the bounds of agreed conduct, Sazonov proceeded to ascribe to her intentions of the most sweeping and ominous kind. Once in control of Constantinople, he argued, she would possess the keys to the Black Sea and Mediterranean, to penetration into Asia Minor and hegemony in the Balkans. By any normal standard, the transition in Russian thinking from the appointment of a German general to a Turkish army post to the establishment of German hegemony over the Near East would surely be considered exaggerated, if not eccentric. It may be that, indeed, German policy, or some Germans, had these objectives. This is not the point. The point is whether Russian decisionmakers in November/December 1913 could arrive at this conclusion on the basis of the available evidence. *Logically* they could not. Even if the von Sanders mission was evidence of German ambitions, it still left German policy far short of its goal. *Psychologically*, if we accept the central importance apparently attached to norms of international conduct and the consequences of their infringement, the Russian conclusion appears far more intelligible. The significance of the appointment went far beyond its ostensible objective. Von Sanders was seen as the thin end of a German wedge to overthrow the existing equilibrium between the powers at Constantinople and to seize control of the Ottoman Empire. And once Germany had infringed the "rules of the game," the entire structure of checks and balances would topple to the ground and an unrestrained scramble for benefits and priviliges in the area would be unleashed, unregulated by the now redundant principle of mutuality. No one could foresee where this struggle might end.

In the crisis of March 1939 both British and Polish decisionmakers harbored the same intriguing sense of grievance about German actions: strange indeed if one considers the actor—Nazi Germany—to whom grievance was attached! All the same, these two parallel examples demonstrate that the norms of behavior at stake at any time need not be of universal application but may be only the perceived property of the relations between the observing and observed actors. For the British government existing norms were defined largely by what were considered to be legitimate German grievances against the Versailles Settlement and, importantly, by the Munich Agreement. Underlying these norms were certain value assumptions about a nation's right to self-determination and the sanctity of promises, even where these possessed no formal, legal status. For the Polish government, as we shall see, relevant norms were defined by quite different principles, peculiar to Polish-German relations.

In the British case the German entry into Prague was seen blatantly and cynically to infringe assurances and promises, some explicit, others informal, personally made by Hitler to the British prime minister at Munich. As Halifax complained to the Cabinet of 15 March 1939, "Germany's attitude in this matter was completely inconsistent with the Munich Agreement. Germany had deliberately preferred naked force to the methods of consultation and discussion." Moreover, the German action was quite incompatible with the "limited" racial and territorial principles which the British government largely accepted: "This was the first occasion on which Germany had applied her shock tactics to the domination of non-Germans . . . it was important to find language which would imply that Germany was now being led on a dangerous path."[12] Identical arguments were put forward by Chamberlain on 17 March 1939 in his Birmingham speech and echoed *ad nauseam* in almost every newspaper and public forum in the country, not least in both Houses of Parliament: Germany had betrayed a trust and overstepped the mark. Even apologists of German revisionism such as Henderson, the British ambassador in Berlin, condemned the "utter cynicism and utter immorality of the whole performance."[13]

The dismemberment of Czechoslovakia was, historians agree almost unanimously, a turning point: the point at which Germany went too far. Until that moment, Nazi Germany had not, it is true, been overattentive to the niceties of diplomatic protocol: the remilitarization of the Rhineland, the *Anschluss*, and Munich had all entailed the use of the most peremptory methods. Nevertheless, Hitler had, all the while, preserved two central norms of conduct: the nationality principle and the fulfilment of commitments voluntarily entered into by the Nazi regime. Germany declared, and Britain tacitly accepted, that the Versailles *diktat* was a dead letter which could not be expected to bind the rulers of the Third Reich. Prague was something quite different.

Once the mark was overstepped, German aims were seen to be menacingly limitless. Halifax, having up till then minimized the extent of German aims, now concluded that the Germans "were seeking to establish a position in which they could by force dominate Europe and, if possible, the world."[14] Chamberlain wondered aloud whether this was "a step in the direction of an attempt to dominate the world by force."[15] With the benefit of hindsight we would probably agree with this estimate of German objectives. But this does not alter the significant psychological point that such an estimate was arrived at as a direct consequence of the German infringement of the "rules of the game" and not before. Liddell Hart, always a perceptive observer, was dismayed by the frantic reaction to events, noting in his diary: "The most ominous aspect of Germany's invasion of Czechoslovakia is not its evidence of her aggressive designs—which should always have been clear enough to anyone before this—but the wave of hysteria it has produced here."[16]

As far as the Polish government was concerned, the operative point about the crisis was not that the Munich Agreement had been breached. Poland was not a signatory to the

agreement, and Beck himself had long considered the days
of Czechoslovakia to be numbered and had even anticipated
Polish gains in the event of its dissolution. The norms governing Polish-German relations were therefore not concerned with guidelines about the sovereign status of
Czechoslovakia. They were based, first of all, on the Non-
Aggression Pact of 1934, secondly on certain assumptions
made by Beck about the Polish sphere of influence which he
believed Germany accepted, and finally on the 1919 settlement which defined the special status of Danzig. Each one
of these principles was broken in turn by the German government. First, as the Poles repeatedly complained, the invasion of Czechoslovakia had been carried out without prior
consultation with the Polish government "in contradiction to
the principles on which the execution of the 1934 Declaration were based."[17] In terms similar to those used by Sazonov
in November 1913 the German government was informed
that "the very fact of placing us in the face of ever new decisions without previous notification does not contribute to the
creation of a good atmosphere in Polish-German relations."[18]

Second, the summary declaration of a German protectorate over Slovakia was particularly disquieting, since Poland
had special and known interests in the area for ethnic, political, and military reasons. Significantly, the first reaction of
the Polish government to the declaration on 16 March 1939
was pointedly to request "a genuine interpretation" of the
arrangement. And in the critical meeting of 21 March with
Ribbentrop, Lipski made an open accusation that the Slovak
protectorate was "directed against Poland." "I emphasized,"
he said, "our community of race, language and religion, and
mentioned the help we had given in their achievement of
independence. I pointed out our long frontier with Slovakia.
I indicated that the Polish man in the street could not understand why the Reich had assumed the protection of Slovakia."[19]

By declaring a protectorate over Slovakia, Germany indeed infringed an implicit verbal assurance given to Poland
recognizing the latter's special interest in the area. On 24

August 1938 Polish ambassador Lipski had discussed, among other things, the future of Czechoslovakia with Reichsmarshall Göring. Following instructions, Lipski argued that his government did "not believe the present Czech creation can exist any longer." He then went on to stress Poland's close ties with Slovakia and her wish for Slovak autonomy. "Göring eagerly confirmed that this is a necessity. He added that Germany is fortunately in such a position that these matters are of no concern to it."[20] In diplomatic language this was a clear renunciation of German interest in favor of Poland.

The final straw was the renewal of German demands for an alteration in the status of Danzig. And on this point there could be no question about Polish rights: these were defined by the Treaty of Versailles, had been jealously defended by the Polish government—not least during Beck's tenure of office—and had been publicly recognized by Hitler (e.g., in November 1937) to be the only basis on which Polish-German relations could rest. To call this situation into question was deliberately to flaunt Polish rights and existing agreements.

As a result of German conduct, Warsaw was plunged into an atmosphere of gloom and foreboding. The German government, especially in its proposals regarding Danzig, had gone past a "Halt!" sign; Danzig, as Pilsudski had taught Beck and Szembek, was a litmus paper of German intentions. Worse still, Hitler knew this only too well; Beck had personally repeated the message to him again and again: "Don't touch Danzig." After 21 March 1939 it seemed clear to Beck (others had seen the light when German troops moved into Slovakia, Bohemia, and Moravia) that the Nazi regime had abandoned existing "rules" of international conduct and was intent on the subjugation of all Europe. In his reasoned exposition of 24 March, Beck argued that Germany, now described as "the enemy," had "lost its calculability" and threatened to violate the limits of the Polish *non possumus*: Polish territorial integrity and her position in Danzig. "A series of new elements" had plunged the situation into "chaos." Germany was on the march across Europe.[21] Others viewed

German intentions even less soberly, and an impending attack was widely anticipated at any moment.

The Soviet proposals of 7 August 1946 infringed recognized norms of behavior in a number of ways. First, point 4 of the Soviet note would have excluded from any future arrangement those signatories of the 1936 convention which were not Black Sea powers. In the American reply to the Soviet note this was the first objection:

> The fourth proposal set forth in the Soviet note does not appear to envisage a revision of the Montreux Convention as suggested in our note to the Turkish Government of November 2, 1945, but rather the establishment of a new regime which would be confined to Turkey and the other Black Sea Powers. It is the view of this Government that the regime of the Straits is a matter of concern not only to the Black Sea Powers but also to other powers, including the United States. This Government cannot, therefore, agree with the Soviet view that the establishment of the regime of the Straits should come under the competence of the Black Sea Powers to the exclusion of other powers.[22]

Although the United States was not a signatory of the Montreux Convention, it was not prepared to acquiesce in the far-reaching structural changes that were proposed. The convention, signed by Great Britain, France, and Japan, as well as by the Black Sea powers themselves, was an expression of the international status of the Straits. The United States could not accept a state of affairs in which the Straits would become, in effect, the special preserve of the Soviet Union and its satellites. American thinking was towards a greater, not a lesser degree of international involvement in waterways such as the Straits.

A second objection was procedural, though with substantive implications: the Soviet note was in breach of the Potsdam Agreement. Instead of proposing a revision of the Montreux Convention, as agreed in the Protocol, it envisaged a "new regime on a fundamentally different basis." Moreover, the Soviet Union made no pretense of following the formal provision laid down in article 29 of the convention allowing for any revision.[23] Instead of proposing a special conference of signatories (the procedure in the event of a failure to reach agreement on the proposed revision through normal diplomatic channels), the Soviet Union was proposing a bilateral arrangement with Turkey. Nor had the proposals been circulated in advance with the signatory powers and an attempt been made to reach prior agreement with these countries. All this may seem to be legalistic and peripheral, but it is not. Soviet failure to abide by the rules of procedure was a clear sign that it considered itself to be in a priviliged position apropos of other states and not bound to respect their interests in the matter. Others were to be kept informed, as a matter of courtesy, but basically had no *locus standi* in the matter. From legal inequality to sphere of influence the step was but a short one.

The final Soviet breach of a "rule" of conduct involved a sin of omission rather than commission. This was the perceived Soviet failure either to take account of the United Nations or to act according to the principles of equality and universality that were supposed to underlie the organization. In its third objection to the Soviet note the American reply observed "that the note of the Soviet Government contains no reference to the United Nations. The position of the Government of the United States is that the regime of the Straits should be brought into appropriate relationship with the United Nations and should function in a manner consistent with the principles and aims of the United Nations."[24] The very idea that the future of a great international waterway should be settled by an unequal and private "deal" between a great power and a minor one was quite opposed to what the United States believed to be the spirit of the United Nations Charter.

As we see from our preceding examples, a breach of "rules of the game" generated certain characteristic responses on the part of the observer: a vision of impending expansion and hegemony and a tendency to exaggerate the significance of the single move at issue. The 1946 incident follows the pattern. Acheson, for instance, saw the Soviet note as a "trial balloon," that is, a maneuver made by the Soviet Union to test the American response: "Acceding to these demands would be followed next by [the] infiltration and domination of Greece by Russia with the obvious consequences in the Middle East and the obvious threat to the line of communications of the British to India." Put in this way, the implications of the Soviet note went far beyond its immediate content. Hence the at first startling conclusion that the proposals "should be firmly resented by the President with the full realization that if Russia did not back down and if we maintained our attitude it might lead to armed conflict." Truman fully accepted this recommendation, justifying his position in sweeping terms: "He was perfectly clear that we should take a firm position both in this instance and in China; that we might as well find out whether the Russians were bent on world conquest now as in five or 10 years."[25] It thus became the accepted view that the Soviet proposals for a revision of the Montreux Convention had the object of subjugating Turkey and of using Turkey as a "springboard"—a popular word—for political and military expansion into the Mediterranean and the Near and Middle East, thereby opening up the way to India and China and eventual world domination. This remarkable vision is suggestive both as a prototype statement of the domino theory and as an example of the fear which accompanied the beginning of the Cold War.

Here, then, is what I believe to be the common link connecting our six different examples of threat perception in international crisis: the appraisal that an observed infringement of accepted norms of international conduct governing relations between the involved parties was the thin end of a wedge of a concerted program of aggression and domination. In the concluding chapter I shall suggest an explanation for this pattern of argument and try to fit this into a wider conceptual framework.

Chapter 14

"Rules" of International Conduct

All communities, whatever their size, from the basic family unit to society as a whole, are obliged to reconcile the sometimes conflicting interests and desires of their members. Failure to contain disagreement within certain bounds makes it difficult to pursue, without interference or distraction, the basic activities of orderly existence. In the worst case the very survival of the community and its members is called into question. Social systems, Talcott Parsons has argued, regulate the behavior of "acting units," and thereby preserve equilibrium within acceptable parameters, through the existence of *values*—generalized conceptions of what is desirable—and *norms*—"which are generalized formulations—more or less explicit—of expectations of proper action by differentiated units in relatively specific situations."[1]

In a rare but extremely suggestive excursion from sociology into international relations, Parsons wonders whether it may not be useful to consider the international system as a type of social system: "Our central problem then may be defined as the need to identify the principal elements of normative order which are present in contemporary international relations, and to suggest their potentialities and limitations for being strengthened at cultural levels and for meeting the basic conditions of minimal institutionalization."[2] Parsons then proceeds to attempt to discover, by empirical observation, what the norms of international behavior might be. He believes that their presence can be discerned, albeit at a primitive level, in the international laws of trade, shipping, and the security of persons, and in the existence of supranational organizations such as the Roman Catholic Church and the U.N. To this somewhat meager list one could add certain assumptions about the illegitimacy of racism, initiated war, and the acquisition of territory by force. At other periods in history, Kal Holsti has pointed out, other normative assumptions have characterized the international system. For instance, in the classical balance-of-power system of the eighteenth and nineteenth centuries, war was permissible only if conducted for limited objectives, not in pursuit of hegemonic goals. Diplomacy was finely regulated by a very precise code of behavior.[3] Morton Kaplan has tried to relate the rules governing conduct between states to the formal structure of the systems of which they are members.[4]

The main difficulty with all these extremely fascinating formulations is that they are presented at such a high level of generalization that it is hard to discern their application in specific instances. The "rules" of conduct governing Soviet-American relations are surely far more precise and specific than the universal norms of Parsons or Kaplan. Both superpowers, no doubt, would denounce racism, initiated war, or the acquisition of territory by force; and occasionally such censensus finds expression in documents or declarations such as UN resolutions 242 and 338 on the Middle East. But over a broad range of issues involving the superpowers, it is clear that their conduct, if it is regulated at all, must be governed by far more concrete principles taking into account factors completely ignored by grand theoreticians—geography, history, technology, domestic structure, and circumstances.

Edward McWhinney, an expert in international law, effectively takes Parsons's argument one step forward. In an analysis of the legal basis of Soviet-American relations, he concludes that in the absence of any single, agreed system of international law (such as existed in the nineteenth century) relations between the superpowers have in fact been governed by a set of tacit "rules of the game" or "ground rules." These include the recognition of each other's spheres of influence, the illegitimacy of nuclear war, and the avoidance of surprises.[5] McWhinney, who wrote in 1964, actually anticipated many of the provisions of the 1972 Soviet-American Agreement on the Basic Principles of Relations, which was an attempt to put the informal rules of détente on a more formal basis.

Where McWhinney differs from Parsons, therefore, is in looking beyond universal norms of behavior for "expectations of proper action" to relatively specific rules of conduct which may be either tacit or explicit and are peculiar to a particular relationship. The "rules" of conduct regulating relations between the superpowers are clearly and necessarily quite different from those governing relations between, say, the United States and a Central American client, a NATO ally, a Soviet satellite, a nonaligned African country, or a member of OPEC.

"Rules of the game," to use McWhinney's (and Schelling's) term—that is, norms of international conduct—can be seen from our case studies to incorporate a broad range of normative concepts, the defining characteristic of which is that they all prescribe the boundaries of permissible behavior: they consist of various kinds of dos and don'ts that guide states in their mutual contact. These "rules" include recognition of the concept of sovereignty—the right of a state to manage, without interference, its own internal affairs (1875); recognition of the legitimacy and territorial integrity of a state (1889); the maintenance of the *status quo* in a given area, whether based on a gentleman's agreement (1913), or as laid down by international treaty (1946); adherence to procedures of consultation in affairs of direct concern to a state, again whether defined by international treaty (1946), by mutual agreement (Britain 1939, Poland 1939), or by some sense of propriety (1913); the right to national self-determination (Britain

1939); the honoring of bilateral agreements (Britian 1939, Poland 1939); the maintenance of privileges defined by international treaty (Poland 1939); and adherence to certain recognized standards of international conduct (Britain 1939, 1946). From this list we can see that "rules of the game" are by no means restricted to the precepts of international law, though they may include them; they can be either specific to a particular relationship or of general application; while sometimes explicitly formulated, they are as often tacit and unwritten.* But the common feature which they share is that they are anticipatory: they entail certain expectations about the future conduct in given circumstances of other actors in the international system. There is nothing logically necessary about such anticipated behavior. (In this sense rules of the game in international relations are quite different from the listed or stipulative rules in bridge or football. In these latter cases the rules define the game, and to infringe them blatantly and systematically is simply to cease playing the game and to court disqualification. In international relations there can be no disqualification of actors or termination of the "game." If anything, the "rules" of international conduct approximate more closely to those understandings or conventions that players develop to settle questions left open by the listed rules.)[6]

Although rules in international relations are not constitutive and therefore not *logically* necessary, neither are they arbitrary or idiosyncratic. In most of our examples decision-makers were well justified in assuming that the opponent was aware of the behavioral norm; indeed, the evidence strongly indicates that this was a correct assumption and that the infringement arose not from ignorance but from a wish to gain unilateral advantage. (Michael Quinn suggests that occasional rule-breaking to gain strategic advantage is quite consistent, as in basketball, with knowledge of the rules and commitment to the game. In fact, cheating is effective only *because* of the prior existence of known rules.)[7] Except for the

---

* Such an eclectic conception of rules has recently been proposed by Hedley Bull, *The Anarchical Society* [London, 1977], chap. 3.

special case of 1889, where the probably mistaken perception of threat arose from an uncritical acceptance of apparently inaccurate information, decisionmakers' expectations were based either on a formal document, a recorded conversation, or an established convention or right. There may be cases where states disagree on, are misinformed about, misinterpret, or misapply rules of conduct. Situations not covered by past agreement or convention may arise. But in the cases examined aggrieved observers could and did appeal to some accepted principle of behavior.

Rules of international conduct, if we are better to understand their function and the consequences of their breach, can be helpfully compared to other practice-defining rules in games, law, morality, and language. One way to look at such rules has been suggested by Thomas Schelling and developed by David Lewis. According to Schelling, tacit ground rules function as a solution to a particular problem of communication which frequently arises: that where participants are required to coordinate or harmonize their behavior without being able to communicate freely or directly. At a trivial level such problems include meeting a friend after a football match after having been separated by the crowd or restoring a telephone connection that has been cut off inadvertently. Similar problems arise in every walk of life, from the setting of fashion trends to price-fixing in an oligopolistic market. They also occur in international relations.

Faced with the problem of coordinating his behavior with that of others in the absence of means of communication, an actor is left with only a single practical alternative: he must attempt to anticipate how those others will behave and act in accordance with such an anticipation. Where many participants are involved—for example, in the stock market—it is only a question of anticipating others' behavior. In normal circumstances there is no possibility of the small speculator by himself affecting others' actions. Where only two, or at least a very limited number of participants are involved, the individual must recognize that he himself constitutes an important factor in the equation. He must therefore take into account what others expect him to do. (There can also be expectations of expectations of expectations—called higher-order expectations—in an infinite regression, but we shall ignore this complicating aspect of the situation as not essential to the main argument.) Thus the problem of tacit communication is soluble on a basis of coordinated expectations, of arriving at anticipations common to those of other participants.

Schelling, to his great credit, recognized and systematically developed the idea that many problems of international, and especially strategic, behavior are structurally very similar to those of everyday life. So it is with the problem of coordinating mutual expectations. For instance, he argues, in questions such as the limit to concession in negotiations and the delineation of international frontiers, some prominent feature of the situation can become a focus for the mutual expectations of the actors. It is also vitally necessary for the Great Powers to agree upon limits to the use of weapons and the scope of belligerency if some local conflict is not to escalate into nuclear war. Since formal agreement may be difficult to reach, it is to tacit ground rules that the actors may have to look.[8]

Schelling intended his theory to apply only to the special case in which participants are obliged to improvise an *ad hoc* and tacit restriction on their freedom of action in order to prevent escalation of conflict when they are unable to communicate freely or directly with each other. According to the linguistic philosopher David Lewis, however, Schelling's special case can be given general application to linguistic convention—the understandings which regulate the use and hence the meaning of words in the language. Conventions, Lewis argues, like tacit ground rules, permit the coordination of behavior by setting up mutual expectations about the linguistic reference of agreed symbols. To some minor extent we do introduce new terms as the need arises (which then become governed by conventions for future use). But on the whole, *prior agreement* on the use of linguistic symbols is a necessary condition for communication at even the most ru-

dimentary level. It would, in practical terms, be quite out of
the question constantly to improvise our means of communication; we cannot make up our language as we go along.
Utter confusion would rapidly result—a Tower of Babel
situation in which coordinated behavior would become
impossible.

Just such an argument can be made for the function of
social rules of conduct as a general class and for rules of
conduct in international relations in particular. Even in
situations where there is no physical impediment to
communication, practical considerations dictate the *prior
existence* of agreement on rules of conduct that can function
as the focus for mutual expectations and, hence, coordinated
behavior:

1. Actors need to know ahead of time what the limits of
permissible behavior are in order to avoid unwitting and potentially disastrous violation of the vital interests of other
parties. Last-minute efforts to reach understanding in the
midst of a rapidly unfolding situation would very likely be
fruitless. Negotiators would find it impossible to keep up
with events; the parties might find that they had already
adopted contradictory positions from which retreat would be
difficult without humiliation. Thus, the pressure of events
might generate an ineluctable momentum over which control would quickly be lost.

2. Agreements between states over the limits of vital interests, rights and commitments cannot simply be impro-
vised but are, in the nature of things, the outcome of often
lengthy and painstaking negotiations. Most areas of inter-
state contact are simply too complicated to allow of easy, off-
the-cuff solutions. States, therefore, must arrive at understandings well ahead of the situations they are intended to
regulate.

3. Rules of conduct—understood limits on action—are
not intended only to regulate eventualities thought likely to
occur. As in the case of defensive agreements, states may
hope not merely to lay down lines of future conduct but also,

by the creation of firm expectations, to prevent the occurrence of those contingencies. This is the deterrent function of rules in international conduct.

Thus linguistic conventions and other kinds of rules of conduct do act as a form of tacit communication even when open communication is theoretically possible. They provide a means for partners in an interaction to read the implications of each other's behavior and act or react accordingly without the need for an accompanying explanation or argument.

Prior agreements on the limits of permitted action in international relations are, like social norms of behavior, a necessity of orderly existence in most situations short of total war or total harmony. Much of the time, for example, actors neither work together nor act in opposition, but are engaged in the routine administration of ongoing concerns that do not entail or require their mutual interaction at the high policy-making level. To permit such coexistence actors must necessarily develop certain principles of behavior to prevent, or at least limit, unwelcome contact. Without these rules relations would continually deteriorate into abrasion and crisis. The international system would be locked in a state of perpetual anarchy in which the slightest collision might lead to war. Established interests could not be maintained and with no reciprocal framework of restraint would be continually threatened. Rules obviate abrasive contact—not always successfully, of course—by inserting a degree of certainty in the relations between states and by permitting most life and contact to be conducted at a routine level, if at all. Hence, states are left free to occupy themselves with what is their essential business most of the time: the management of their domestic affairs and the administration of ongoing interests.

The most obvious examples of such "routinization" are provided by international law in a limited number of areas, such as the rights of foreign nationals, shipping, foreign trade, and so on. The very success of international law in these areas is attested to by the frequent charge that it deals only with the noncontroversial. Such subjects, about which wars

were once fought, are now noncontroversial precisely because of the success of international law in setting up clear—
and mutually beneficial—ground rules of behavior.

The best way to coordinate the mutual expectations of
actors is, as we learn from international law, by universal,
specific, and generally accepted rules of conduct. Another
good way is by prior contingency agreement. As we see from
our case studies, expectations about behavior often derive
from a formal agreement such as the Polish-German Ten-
Year Pact of 1934 or the Potsdam Agreement of 1945. Explicit
agreement, however, may not always be possible. There are
a number of reasons for this. Most obviously, explicit ar-
rangements cannot possibly be made to cover all contingencies. And then, even if it were technically possible to foresee
all contingencies, negotiation between adversaries would
still raise numerous and interminable difficulties, some of
them insuperable. Factors such as domestic and alliance
opinion, bureaucratic in-fighting, and concern for prestige
would all hinder agreement. Where explicit agreement and
international law are not available as foci of expectations, a
third possibility arises. In recurrent situations (unique situations raise different problems) coordination can also be
achieved by adhering to recognized and regular patterns of
behavior—"conventions," in Lewis's terminology. These have
two possible sources: tradition and informal understanding.
Conventions are not only a substitute for formal agreement.
They may also possess clear advantages: they do not pin
down the prestige of the actors in changing circumstances
that may require them to reassess their positions; they do not
raise the negotiating problems often involved in formal
agreements; they are less embarrassing, can be publicly denied, and bypass the bureaucratic process and alliance partners. Their clear disadvantage as compared to formal
agreements is that they may very well be imprecise, misun-
derstood, or contradictory. By their very nature they are subjective and, as we have seen, sometimes contain an element
of wishful thinking.

This discussion has put us in a position to account for the

association between perceptions of threat and infringements of the "rules of the game" and to provide an overall explanation of why threat should be perceived at all. The key to the puzzle lies in the Schelling-Lewis theory of the coordination of mutual expectations. Let us, therefore, consider the consequences, in terms of the model, of infringements of the rules. To simplify matters, let us assume that we are dealing solely with a two-actor situation.

A. It will be recalled that the function of prior agreement, whether formal or informal, is to enable actors to harmonize their behavior in a situation in which they are unable to communicate with each other or in which it would be impractical for them constantly to have to do so. By conforming to rules mutually understood, they obviate the risk of collision and unnecessary conflict. Without such rules it would be impossible to prevent the system's breaking down into anarchy. Now international relations, if it is nothing else, is an ongoing process of transaction and mutual accommodation. This recurrent nature of international relations has at least one important implication: it raises any single example of interaction between states beyond the level of a momentary encounter to a learning situation with implications for any future transaction in the continuing process. Once this is understood to be the case, the far-reaching effect of the failure of a given actor to keep to the rules becomes apparent. By infringing the norms an actor disappoints expectations. His behavior becomes unforeseeable. And inability to predict that actor's behavior critically disrupts the possibility of harmonizing one's own actions with his in a situation in which negotiations are ruled out, as they often will be. At stake in an infringement of "rules of the game" is the possibility of tacit communication. When this becomes impossible, both parties are condemned to a *dialogue des sourds*. In this situation coordination is ruled out and relations between the actors plunge into that state of uncertainty, previously avoided, that is the prelude to chaos. The threatening prospect at hand goes far beyond the immediate conse-

quences of the infringement and extends to the future state
of the international system.

B. A rule, I have argued, enables actors to coordinate their
behavior by providing a focus for their mutual expectations.
We can call this the signpost function of "rules of the game."
Rules point the way to a predetermined rendezvous. If the
signpost should be knocked down or altered, travelers jour-
neying apart will be unable to arrive at a common destina-
tion; coordinated behavior becomes impossible. But rules
also perform a second, complementary boundary function:
they demarcate the territory of the permissible from that of
the forbidden. And just as an infringement of "rules of the
game" removes the only means of tacit communication between actors, it also removes the only means for tacit restraint between them. After the frontier has been crossed,
there is no other plausible line of demarcation to fall back
on. The boundary was created, whether informally or explicitly, as a mutually recognized and recognizable limitation of
actors' behavior; beyond it, as Schelling points out in a discussion of physical frontiers, "there is just no other stopping
place that can be tacitly acknowledged by other sides."[9] At
this point the calculus of mutual expectations reenters the
picture. Since the boundary—the inhibition—marks the only
agreed restraint on action, the victim will understand the infringement as a statement of intent by his opponent to proceed further. The infractor, the victim will go on to argue,
must be well aware that beyond the boundary there is no
other agreed stopping place. He knows that the infringement
will not be seen as a purely limited operation and that he can
expect to meet with forceful opposition. Understanding the
implications of his infringement, the infractor would have
undertaken it only if he was prepared from the beginning to
risk conflict. Therefore, the victim will conclude, the infractor's action can only be interpreted as a challenge to the existing balance of relations as a whole. If we combine this
aspect of infringement with that put forward under A, it will
be readily seen that the infringement takes on the aspect not
just of a limited attempt to achieve immediate gain, but of an

event of far-reaching significance, an ominous warning of impending danger to the entire structure of international order of which the observer, the victim, is a part.

Threat perception, then, is the product of a deductive heuristic—a cognitive "rule of thumb"—made use of by decisionmakers in situations of uncertainty about the intentions of other actors. In the concluding paragraphs of this study it is appropriate to refer back to an example of threat appraisal taken from one of our case studies. It is worth quoting at length because it exemplifies so well the cognitive logic that associates impending danger with a perceived violation of agreed "rules" of international conduct. The analysis is that of Colonel Beck on 21 March 1939:

> The situation is serious . . . because one of the elements hitherto timely for the definition of the state's situation, that is, Germany, *has lost its calculability. . . . We defined with precision the limits of our direct interest,* and beyond this line we conduct a normal policy. . . . *Below this line comes our Polish non possumus.* This is clear: we will fight. Once the matter is put this way, *chaos is overcome by a considerable share of calm,* and thinking becomes orderly. Where is the line? It is our territory, but not only that. The line also involves the nonacceptance by our state, regarding the drastic spot that Danzig has always been, of any unilateral suggestion to be imposed on us. And, regardless of what Danzig is worth as an object . . . under the present circumstances *it has become a symbol.* This means that, *if we join that category of eastern states that allow rules to be dictated to them, then I do not know where the matter will end.*[10]

Within any structure of relations which it is desired to preserve, certain "rules of the game" will be developed to regulate permissible behavior between the actors. In a dangerously uncertain world they allow a minimal degree of certainty. But they are like a seamless web. Damaged at one point, the whole fabric threatens to disintegrate. Threat, then, is like a tug on this web of rules, its perception an anticipation of a descent into disorder and uncertainty. And chaos, as any biologist knows, is the ultimate abhorrence of sentient organisms.

Notes/Index

Abbreviations

BD   *British Documents on the Origins of the War, 1898–1914.* Ed. G. P. Gooch and H. Temperley, Vol. 9, London, 1934; Vol. 10, London, 1936.

DBFP   *Documents on British Foreign Policy, 1919–1939.* Ed. E. L. Woodward and R. Butler. 3rd ser. Vols. 2–5. London, 1949–52.

DDF   *Documents diplomatiques français, 1871–1914.* 1st ser.: Vol. 1, Paris, 1929; Vol. 7, Paris, 1937. 3rd ser.: Vol. 4, Paris, 1932; Vol. 8, Paris, 1935.

DDI   *I documenti diplomatici italiani.* 2nd ser. Vol. 21. Rome, 1968.

FRUS   *Foreign Relations of the United States. 1939,* Vol. 1, Washington, D.C., 1956. *1945,* Vol. 8, Washington, D.C., 1969. *1946,* Vols. 1, 2, 6, 7, Washington, D.C., 1969–72.

GP   *Die grosse Politik der europäischen Kabinette, 1871–1914.* Ed. J. Lepsius, A. Mendelsohn Bartholdy, F. Thimme. Vol. 1, Berlin, 1927. Vol. 6, Berlin, 1927. Vol. 34, Berlin, 1926. Vol. 38, Berlin, 1926.

PRO, Cab. Public Records Office, Cabinet Series, London.

PRO, FO Public Records Office, Foreign Office Series, London.

PWB   *Official Documents Concerning Polish-German and Polish-Soviet Relations, 1933–1939 (The Polish White Book).* London, 1940.

Notes

Chapter 1: Threat Perception

1 C. Hermann, "International Crisis as a Situational Variable," in *International Politics and Foreign Policy*, ed. J. N. Rosenau, rev. ed. (New York, 1969), pp. 411–16.

2 M. Brecher, "Towards a Theory of International Crisis Behavior," *International Studies Quarterly* 21 (March 1977): 43–44; G. H. Snyder and P. Diesing, *Conflict among Nations* (Princeton, 1977), p. 6.

3 K. Knorr, "Threat Perception," in *Historical Dimensions of National Security Problems*, ed. K. Knorr (Lawrence, Kansas, 1976), p. 78.

4 Quoted by T. W. Milburn, "The Nature of Threat," *Journal of Social Issues* 33 (1977): 126.

5 D. A. Baldwin, "Thinking about Threats," *Journal of Conflict Resolution* 15 (1971): 71–78.

6 C. Lockhart, *The Efficacy of Threats in International Interaction Strategies*, Sage International Studies Series 2 (Beverly Hills, 1973).

7 Knorr, "Threat Perception."

8 J. D. Singer, "Threat-Perception and the Armament Tension Dilemma," *Journal of Conflict Resolution* 2, no. 1 (1958): 93–94.

9 See W. Platt, *Strategic Intelligence Production* (New York, 1957), pp. 61–62.

10 T. C. Schelling, *The Strategy of Conflict* (Cambridge, Mass., 1960).

11 D. G. Pruitt, "Definition of the Situation as a Determinant of International Action," in *International Behavior*, ed. H. G. Kelman (New York, 1965), pp. 399–407.

12 For example, the following hypothesis is tested: "If a state's perception of injury (or frustration, dissatisfaction, hostility or threat) to itself is sufficiently great, this perception will offset perceptions of insufficient capability, making the perception of capability much less important a factor in a decision to go to war" (D. A. Zinnes, et al., "Capability, Threat, and the Outbreak of War," in Rosenau, *International Politics and Foreign Policy*, 1st ed. [New York, 1961], pp. 469–82). Also see D. A. Zinnes et al.,

"The Expression and Perception of Hostility in Prewar Crisis: 1914," in *Quantitative International Politics*, ed. J. D. Singer (New York, 1968), pp. 85–119.

13 R. A. Brody et al., "Hostile International Communication, Arms Production, and Perception of Threat: A Simulation Study," *Peace Research Society (International) Papers* 7 (1967): 15–40.

14 Lockhart, *The Efficacy of Threats*, pp. 44–45.

15 Knorr, "Threat Perception," pp. 78–119.

16 J. Steinberg, "The Copenhagen Complex," *Journal of Contemporary History* 1 (1966): 23–46.

17 U. Bialer, *The Shadow of the Bomber* (London: The Royal Historical Society, 1979).

18 I. L. Janis, "Psychological Effects of Warnings," in *Man and Society in Disaster*, ed. G. W. Baker and D. W. Chapman (New York, 1962), pp. 69–71.

19 S. B. Withey, "Sequential Accommodations to Threat," in *The Threat of Impending Disaster*, ed. G. H. Grosser et al. (New York, 1962), pp. 69–71.

20 G. Hecksher, "General Methodological Problems," in *Comparative Politics: A Reader*, ed. H. Eckstein and D. E. Apter (New York, 1963), pp. 35–43.

Chapter 2: The Methodology of Comparative Analysis

1 H. Eckstein, "Case Study and Theory in Political Science," in *Handbook of Political Science*, ed. F. I. Greenstein and N. W. Polsby, (Reading, Mass., 1975): 81–85.

2 S. Verba, "Some Dilemmas in Comparative Research," *World Politics*, 20, no. 1 (October 1967): 111–15; A. L. George and R. Smoke, *Deterrence in American Foreign Policy: Theory and Practice* (New York, 1974), pp. 95–97.

3 J. S. Mill, *A System of Logic* (1843; London, 1963).

4 E. Durkheim, The Rules of Sociological Method (New York, 1938), p. 130.

5 M. Fortes and E. E. Evans-Pritchard, eds., *African Political Systems* (London, 1940). For a helpful survey of the comparative approach see S. N. Eisenstadt, "Social Institutions: Comparative Study," in *International Encyclopedia of the Social Sciences*, 14 (New York and London, 1968): 421–28.

6 Preface to Fortes and Evans-Pritchard, *African Political Systems*, p. 1.

7 N. Smelser, "Notes on the Methodology of Comparative Analy-

sis of Economic Activity," *Social Science Information* 6, nos. 2–3 (1967): 16.

8 George and Smoke, *Deterrence in American Foreign Policy*, p. 91.

9 Social Science Research Council, "Research in Comparative Politics," *American Political Science Review* 47, no. 3 (1953): 647.

10 Ibid., p. 656.

11 A counterclaim is made by P. J. McGowan and H. B. Shapiro, *The Comparative Study of Foreign Policy: A Survey of Scientific Findings* (Beverly Hills and London, 1973).

12 J. N. Rosenau, "Comparative Foreign Policy: Fad, Fantasy, or Field?" *International Studies Quarterly* 12, no. 3 (1968): 300. Also see D. J. Puchala, "Foreign Policy Analysis and Beyond," *Comparative Politics* 2, no. 3 (1970): 501–2.

13 S. P. Huntington, "Arms Races: Prerequisites and Results," in *Approaches to Measurement in International Relations*, ed. J. E. Mueller (New York, 1969), pp. 15–33; B. M. Russett, "The Calculus of Deterrence," *Journal of Conflict Resolution* 7, no. 2 (1963): 97–109; A. Dowty, "The Application of International Guarantees to the Egypt-Israel Conflict," ibid. 16, no. 2 (1972): 253–67; A. Dowty, "Conflict in War-Potential Politics: An Approach to Historical Macroanalysis," *Peace Research Society (International) Papers* 13 (1969): 85–103; O. R. Young, *The Politics of Force* (Princeton, 1968); George and Smoke, *Deterrence in American Foreign Policy*.

14 A. Lijphart, "Comparative Politics and the Comparative Method," *American Political Science Review* 65, no. 3 (September 1971): 686.

15 Ibid, pp. 688–89.

16 See, for example, G. Liska, *Nations in Alliance* (Baltimore, 1962); R. Jervis, *The Logic of Images in International Relations* (Princeton, 1970).

17 R. Marsh, *Comparative Sociology* (New York, 1967), p. 22.

18 Young, *The Politics of Force*.

19 A. Etzioni, *Political Unification* (New York, 1965).

20 Preface to Fortes and Evans-Pritchard, *African Political Systems*, p. 1.

21 G. Sjoberg, "The Comparative Method in the Social Sciences," in *Comparative Perspectives: Theories and Methods*, ed. A. Etzioni and F. Dubow (Boston, 1970), p. 24.

22 R. S. Lazarus, *Psychological Stress and the Coping Process* (New York, 1966), p. 25.
23 On this, see Eckstein, "Case Study and Theory in Political Science," pp. 100–104.
24 George and Smoke, *Deterrence in American Foreign Policy*, p. 96.
25 A. Lijphart, "The Comparable-Cases Strategy in Comparative Research," *Comparative Political Studies* 8 (July 1975): 158–77.

Chapter 3: France and the "War in Sight" Crisis of 1875
1 Vicomte de Gontaut-Biron, *Mon ambassade en Allemagne, 1872–1873* (Paris, 1906), pp. 38, 69–71, 123, 305.
2 W. L. Langer, *European Alliances and Alignments, 1871–1890* (New York, 1950), pp. 36–38.
3 Lord Newton, *Lord Lyons*, II (London, 1913), 41, Russell to Lyons, 14 March 1873.
4 G. Hanotaux, *Contemporary France* II (London, 1905), 100–104, 485–93; Ibid., III (1907), 60–61.
5 *DDF*, 1st ser., I, no. 246, Decazes circular dispatch, 7 December 1873; no. 299, Decazes to Rochefoucauld-Bisaccia, 29 April 1874.
6 Gontaut-Biron, *Mon ambassade*, p. 105.
7 *DDF*, 1st ser., I, no. 251, Gontaut-Biron to Decazes, 26 December 1873; nos. 295 and 308, Decazes circular dispatches, 27 March and 17 July 1874; no. 340, Gontaut-Biron to Decazes, 30 October 1874.
8 *DDF*, 1st ser., I, no. 359, de Savye to Decazes, 5 March 1875; no. 360, Decazes to de Corcelle, 5 March 1875; no. 362, Decazes to de Jarnac, 6 March 1875.
9 *DDF*, 1st ser., I, nos. 365 and 368, de Savye to Decazes, 7 and 9 March 1875.
10 Newton, *Lord Lyons*, II, 68–69, Lyons to Derby, 12 March 1875.
11 *DDF*, 1st ser., I, no. 370, Decazes to de Faverney, 12 March 1875.
12 Newton, *Lord Lyons*, II, 70–71, Lyons to Derby, 16 March 1875.
13 *DDF*, 1st ser., I, no. 373, de Faverney to Decazes, 25 March 1875.
14 H. Wereszycki, "Alarm wojenny 1875 roku, w swietle niewyzskanych zrodel" [The war scare of 1875 in the light of previously unexploited sources], *Kwartalnik Historyczny* 68 (1961): 689–716.

15 *DDF*, 1st ser., I, no. 374, d'Harcourt to Decazes, 2 April 1875.
16 *DDF*, 1st ser., I, no. 375, Decazes circular dispatch, 3 April 1875.
17 Ibid; Hanotaux, *Contemporary France*, III, 212, Decazes to d'Harcourt, 9 April 1875.
18 PRO, FO, 27/2107/291, Lyons to Derby, 5 April 1875.
19 Hanotaux, *Contemporary France*, III, 217.
20 On 13 March the National Assembly passed the third reading of a law which provided for the addition of a fourth battallion to every regiment.
21 *GP*, I, no. 160n.
22 Hanotaux, *Contemporary France*, III, 212, Decazes to d'Harcourt, 9 April 1875.
23 *GP*, I, no. 160n.
24 *GP*, I, no. 160, Hohenlohe to Foreign Office, 10 April 1875; no. 164, Hohenlohe to Bismarck, 12 April 1875.
25 Newton, *Lord Lyons*, II, 72, Adams to Lyons.
26 *GP*, I, no. 164, Hohenlohe to Bismarck, 12 April 1875.
27 Hanotaux, *Contemporary France*, III, 216, Decazes to de Noailles, 10 April 1875.
28 Ibid., p. 220, Decazes to Le Flô, 14 April 1875.
29 Ibid.
30 H. S. Blowitz, *My Memoirs* (London, 1903), pp. 106–9.
31 *DDF*, 1st ser., I, no. 395, Gontaut-Biron to Decazes, 21 April 1875.
32 A. Dreux, *Dernières années de l'ambassade en Allemagne de M. de Gontaut-Biron: 1874–1877* (Paris, 1907), pp. 98–99, Gontaut-Biron to Decazes, 24 April 1875.
33 PRO, FO, 27/2107/339, Adams to Derby, 26 April 1875.
34 Blowitz, *My Memoirs*, pp. 110–13.
35 *DDF*, 1st ser., I, no. 399, Decazes circular dispatch, 29 April 1875.
36 Dreux, *Dernières années*, pp. 100–103, Decazes to Gontaut-Biron, 29 April 1875.
37 *Krasny Arkhiv*, VI, no. 91 (Moscow, 1938), 123–24, Orlov to Gorchakov, 29 April 1875.
38 *GP*, I, no. 169, Hohenlohe to Bismarck, 29 April 1875.
39 Dreux, *Dernières années*, pp. 100–103, Decazes to Gontaut-Biron, 29 April 1875; *DDF*, 1st ser., I, no. 399, Decazes to Gontaut-Biron, 29 April 1875.
40 *DDF*, 1st ser., I, no. 402, Decazes to Gontaut-Biron, 6 May 1875.
41 PRO, FO, 27/2108/368–371, Adams to Derby, 5 May 1875.
42 *DDF*, 1st ser., I, no. 403, Gavard to Decazes, 6 May 1875.

43 *DDF*, 1st ser., I, no. 404, Le Flô to Decazes, 6 May 1875.
44 W. Taffs, "The War Scare of 1875," *Slavonic and East European Review* 9 (1930–31): 641–42.
45 Hanotaux, *Contemporary France*, III, 243–44, Decazes to Gontaut-Biron, 8 May 1875.
46 *DDF*, 1st ser., I, no. 428, Decazes circular dispatch, 18 May 1875.
47 Hanotaux, *Contemporary France*, III, 252, Decazes to Gontaut-Biron, 14 May 1875. Decazes was referring here to a view put forward by Gontaut-Biron on more than one occasion that it was Moltke and the General Staff rather than Bismarck who were behind the spate of rumors.

Chapter 4: The Italian Invasion Scare of July 1889
 1 *The Memoirs of Francesco Crispi*, ed. T. Palamenghi-Crispi, II (London, 1912), 194–204 (henceforth *Crispi Memoirs*).
 2 G. Salvemini, *La politica estera di Francesco Crispi* (Rome, 1919), p. 40.
 3 *DDI*, XXI, nos. 651 and 703, Crispi to Menabrea, 7 and 27 March 1888; *DDF*, 1st ser., VII, no. 177, de Moüy to Goblet, 14 July 1888; no. 189, Goblet to Herbette, 31 July 1889.
 4 Palamenghi-Crispi, *Crispi Memoirs*, II, 306ff.
 5 Ibid., pp. 277, 278, 285, 313–14, 349.
 6 *DDI*, XXI, no. 104, Boselli to Crispi, 5 September 1887; no. 126, Crispi to Ressmann, 10 September 1887; no. 144, de Launay to Crispi, 14 September 1887; nos. 327, 378, and 473, Crispi to Catalini, 20 November and 5 December 1887, 1 January 1888.
 7 *DDF*, 1st ser., VII, no. 69, 6 March 1888, Waddington to Goblet; Lady G. Cecil, *Life of Robert, Marquis of Salisbury*, IV (London, 1932), 103.
 8 Salvemini, *Politica estera*, pp. 41–47; A. C. Jemolo, *Crispi* (Florence, 1922), pp. 35ff.
 9 W. L. Langer, *European Alliances and Alignments, 1871–1890* (New York, 1950), pp. 394, 400–405.
10 C. W. Seton-Watson, *Italy from Liberalism to Fascism, 1870–1925* (London, 1967), pp. 124, 132.
11 *DDI*, XXI, nos. 346, 347, memorandum, 27 November 1887.
12 A. J. Marder, *British Naval Policy, 1880–1905: The Anatomy of British Sea Power* (London, 1940), pp. 126–28; *DDI*, XXI, no. 516, Catalini to Crispi, 23 January 1888; no. 539, Crispi to Catalini, 1 February 1888; no. 548, de Launay to Crispi, 3 February 1888.

13 *GP*, VI, no. 1278, Solms to Foreign Office, 5 March 1888.
14 Quoted in Marder, *British Naval Policy*, pp. 142–43.
15 *GP*, VI, no. 1318, Bismarck to Solms, 2 March 1889; no. 1319, Solms to Bismarck, 10 March 1889. On 28 March 1889, Solms wrote to Bismarck: "The Italian Navy sees that if it were forced to engage France at sea by itself, then it would have little chance of victory, in spite of the superiority of its ironclads" (*GP*, VI, no. 1321).
16 Palamenghi-Crispi, *Crispi Memoirs*, II, 389–91, Crispi to Bertole, 19 April 1889.
17 Salvemini, *Politica estera*, pp. 49–54.
18 Langer, *European Alliances*, pp. 432–33.
19 E. L. Woodward, "The Diplomacy of the Vatican under Popes Pius IX & Leo XIII," *Journal of the British Institute of International Affairs* 3 (1924): 129–30.
20 Seton-Watson, *Italy from Liberalism to Fascism*, pp. 122–23.
21 On becoming foreign minister, Crispi defined his aims as twofold: in the short term, peace; in the longer term, adjustment of Europe on nationalist principles (*DDI*, XXI, no. 57, Crispi to Blanc, 18 August 1887).
22 Palamenghi-Crispi, *Crispi Memoirs*, II, 171–79.
23 Langer, *European Alliances*, pp. 400–404.
24 Palamenghi-Crispi, *Crispi Memoirs*, II, 380–85.
25 Ibid., p. 396.
26 A. Marsden, *British Diplomacy and Tunis, 1875–1902* (London, 1971), pp. 95–109.
27 This was the first time such a summons had been given during the pontificate of Leo XIII. His predecessor had resorted to it only once (PRO, FO, 45/624/146, Dering to Salisbury, 3 July 1889).
28 Ibid.; PRO, FO, 45/624/150, Dering to Salisbury, 7 July 1889.
29 PRO, FO, 45/622/163, Salisbury to Dering, 24 July 1889; PRO, FO, 45/624/159, Dering to Salisbury, 23 July 1889.
30 Palamenghi-Crispi, *Crispi Memoirs*, II, 393.
31 Ibid., pp. 392–93. A story on the same lines appeared in the semiofficial *Riforma* on 11 July. The situation, it argued, was far from reassuring, and peace was placed in danger day by day (quoted in the *Times* [London], 12 July 1889).
32 D. Farini, *Diario di fine secolo*, II (Rome, 1961), p. 1533, entry for 12 July 1889.
33 Palamenghi-Crispi, *Crispi Memoirs*, II, 395, Crispi diary entry, 16 July 1889.

34 G. Giolitti, *Memoirs of My Life* (London, 1923), p. 59.
35 Quoted in the *Times* (London), 13 July 1889. My emphasis.
36 PRO, FO, 45/622/162, Salisbury to Dering, 24 July 1889; Pala-
      menghi-Crispi, *Crispi Memoirs*, II, 407–8, Cucchi to Crispi, 21
      July 1889.
37 Palamenghi-Crispi, *Crispi Memoirs*, II, 394–97, diary entries,
      12–20 July 1889.
38 PRO, FO, 45/622/162, Salisbury to Dering, 24 July 1889.
39 Palamenghi-Crispi, *Crispi Memoirs*, II, 394, diary entry, 14 July
      1889; p. 395, diary entry, 16 July 1889; PRO, FO, 45/624/160,
      Dering to Salisbury, 23 July 1889.
40 Palamenghi-Crispi, *Crispi Memoirs*, II, 395–96, diary entry, 16
      July 1889; PRO, FO, 45/622/162, Salisbury to Dering, 24 July
      1889.
41 PRO, FO, 45/622/162, Salisbury to Dering, 24 July 1889; 45/624/
      158, Dering to Salisbury, 22 July 1889; 45/622/159, Salisbury to
      Dering, 24 July 1889.
42 PRO, FO, 45/624/158, Dering to Salisbury, 22 July 1889; 45/624/
      160, Dering to Salisbury, 23 July 1889. On 22 July two interest-
      ing articles, "known to be inspired from the Italian Foreign Of-
      fice," appeared in the Rome press. *Il Popolo Romano* described
      the condition of the Balkan states as "a continual menace to
      European peace" and expressed the opinion that Russian re-
      sentment of the Bulgarian situation and the hopes of the Pan-
      slavist party with regard to Serbia constituted a "great danger
      to the peace of Europe." *Il Riforma* pointed out "the disasters
      which the Papacy would bring on itself were it unsuccessfully
      to attempt to restore the temporal power with the help of for-
      eign arms" (clippings enclosed in PRO, FO, 45/624/161). At the
      same time Crispi was warning the pope directly of the conse-
      quences of his leaving the Vatican (Palamenghi-Crispi, *Crispi
      Memoirs*, II, 400, diary entry, 21 July 1889; ibid., pp. 401–7).
43 PRO, FO, 45/624/159, Dering to Salisbury, 23 July 1889.
44 Palamenghi-Crispi, *Crispi Memoirs*, II, 407–8, Cucchi to Crispi,
      21 July 1889; ibid., p. 411, Cucchi to Crispi, 24 July 1889.
45 PRO, FO, 45/625/165, Dering to Salisbury, 1 August 1889.

Chapter 5: Russia and the Liman von Sanders Affair of 1913
1 Baron M. de Taube, *La Politique russe d'avant-guerre* (Paris,
      1928), pp. 276, 297–99.
2 *GP*, XXXVIII, 152, Kühlmann to Bethmann-Hollweg, 16 October

1913. See R. H. Davidson, "The Armenian Crisis, 1912–1914," *American Historical Review* 53 (1948): 500.

3 On German influence in the Near East, see M.S. Anderson, *The Eastern Question* (London, 1966), pp. 264ff. On Russian ambivalence to German culture and achievement, see W. Laqueur, *Russia and Germany* (London, 1965), pp. 39–50.

4 A. N. Mandelstam, "La Politique russe d'accès à la Mediterranée au XXᵉ siècle," *Académie de Droit International, Recueil des Cours* 47, no. 1 (1934): 796, 607.

5 In 1900 the Baghdad Railway scheme prompted a warning from Russian Foreign Minister Mouraviev to the czar that Germany could not be allowed "to play a preponderant role on the banks of the Bosphorus, where we have unchallangeable historical tasks." An occupation of the Bosphorus by any power other than Russia "would present Russia with innumerable dangers" (ibid., pp. 633–35).

6 Anderson, *The Eastern Question*, p. 288.

7 B. von Siebert, ed., *Graf Benckendorffs diplomatischer Schriftwechsel* (Berlin, 1928), III, 187, Sazonov to Benckendorff, 1 May 1913.

8 Anderson, *The Eastern Question*, pp. 288, 294.

9 *DDF*, 3rd ser., IV, no. 311, Louis to Poincaré, 2 November 1912.

10 Taube, *Politique russe d'avant-guerre*, p. 303.

11 Ibid., pp. 306–7.

12 Siebert, *Benckendorffs diplomatischer Schriftwechsel*, III, 190, Giers to Sazonov, 10 May 1913.

13 Ibid., p. 186, Sazonov to Benckendorff, 1 May 1913.

14 *Times* (London), 2 July 1913.

15 S. Sazonov, *Fateful Years: 1909–1916* (New York, 1928), p. 117.

16 *Un Livre noir*, II (Paris, 1922–23), p. 362, Sazonov memorandum, 6 November 1913.

17 Details of the mission were apparently reported in the Berlin press as early as 30 October (*DDF*, 3rd ser., VIII, no. 411). On 30 October the British ambassador in Constantinople learned of the mission directly from the German ambassador (*BD*, X, no. 376).

18 *Materialy po franko-russikh otnoshenii za 1910–1914 gg* (Moscow, 1922), pp. 631–32, Giers to Sazonov, 2 and 5 November 1913.

19 *GP*, XXXVIII, 206, Lucius to Foreign Office, 7 November 1913.

20 *Materialy po franko-russikh otnoshenii*, p. 632, Neratov to Sverbeev, 7 November 1913.

21 *GP*, XXXVIII, 207–8, Lucius to Foreign Office, 11 November
    1913. Lucius also used the telling argument that Russia had no
    objection to the English naval mission (which was engaged in
    strengthening the Turkish Navy).
22 *Materialy po franko-russikh otnoshenii*, p. 633, Sazonov to
    Sverbeev, 10 November 1913.
23 In a letter of 14 November Giers made the point that the main
    significance of the mission lay in its "political aspect." The Ger-
    mans claimed that their presence "could contribute to the
    maintenance of the *status quo*; this was hardly part of the im-
    mediate role of a general whose task was the instruction of
    troops" (*Livre noir*, II, 173–74).
24 *GP*, XXXVIII, 208–9, Lucius to Foreign Office, 17 November
    1913.
25 V. N. Kokovtsov, *Out of My Past* (New York, 1934), p. 384.
26 *Livre noir*, II, 413–14, Kokovtsov's report to czar, 2 December
    1913.
27 *GP*, XXXVIII, 216, Bethmann-Hollweg's notes, 18 November 1913.
    After the meeting Kokovtsov commented to the Turkish ambas-
    sador that it was "not the agreement but also the manner in
    which it had been concluded" that demanded Russia's atten-
    tion (Kokovtsov, *Out of My Past*, p. 387).
28 *GP*, XXXVIII, 216–17, Bethmann-Hollweg's notes, 19 November
    1913.
29 *DDF*, 3rd ser., VIII, no. 521, Delcassé to Pichon, 24 November
    1913; *Livre noir*, II, 412, Kokovtsov's report to czar, 2 December
    1913.
30 Siebert, *Benckendorffs diplomatischer Schriftwechsel*, III, 207,
    Sazonov to Benckendorff, 25 November 1913.
31 *BD*, x, no. 380, O'Beirne to Grey, 26 November 1913.
32 *GP*, XXXVIII, 234–35, von Wangenheim to Foreign Office, 4 and
    5 December 1913; p. 239, Pourtales to Foreign Office, 6 De-
    cember 1913. On 11 December Sazonov spoke to British Chargé
    d'Affaires O'Beirne "with greater seriousness and openness
    than on any other occasion that I can remember. He says that
    he does not attach great importance to [the military mission's]
    purely military aspect. General von Sanders may very likely
    not be more successful with the Turkish Army than was von
    der Goltz [his predecessor]. But he is firmly convinced that the
    command of the First Army Corps will give Germany such a
    complete political preponderance at Constantinople that other
    Powers will find themselves reduced to a secondary position in

Turkey" (*BD*, x, no. 418, O'Beirne to Grey, 11 December 1913).

33 *Livre noir*, ii 363–73, Sazonov memorandum, 6 December 1913.

34 Siebert, *Benckendorffs diplomatischer Schriftwechsel*, iii, 209, Sazonov to Benckendorff, 7 December 1913. The note was never delivered, though England, France, and Russia submitted a joint questionnaire to Turkey on 13 December.

35 R. J. Kerner, "The Mission of Liman von Sanders; Part IV," *Slavonic and East European Review* 7 (1928–29): 95.

Chapter 6: Britain and the Prague Crisis of March 1939

1 *DBFP*, ii, app. to no. 1228.

2 K. Feiling, *Life of Neville Chamberlain* (London, 1946), p. 367.

3 J. W. Wheeler-Bennett, *Munich: Prologue to Tragedy* (London, 1948), p. 314.

4 *DBFP*, iii, no. 325, Anglo-French conversations, 24 November 1938.

5 D. Dilks, ed., *The Diaries of Sir Alexander Cadogan, 1938– 1945* (London, 1971), p. 114 (henceforth *Cadogan Diaries*).

6 In the Vienna Award of 2 November 1938. See R. G. D. Laffan et al., *Survey of International Affairs 1938*, iii (London: RIIA, 1953), 68–112.

7 *DBFP*, iii, no. 285, Halifax to Phipps, 1 November 1938.

8 Feiling, *Neville Chamberlain*, p. 392.

9 Dilks, *Cadogan Diaries*, pp. 130, 139; I. Colvin, *The Chamberlain Cabinet* (London, 1971), p. 181.

10 *DBFP*, iv, app. 1, sec. iii, 19 February 1939, Chamberlain to Henderson; sec. iv, 20 February 1939, Halifax to Henderson.

11 Feiling, *Neville Chamberlain*, pp. 396–97; Lord Halifax, *Fulness of Days* (London, 1957), p. 232.

12 Dilks, *Cadogan Diaries*, p. 116; B. H. Liddell Hart, *Memoirs*, ii (London, 1965), 172ff.; R. J. Minney, *The Private Papers of Hore-Belisha* (London, 1960), p. 146, notes, 24 September 1938.

13 *DBFP*, iii, no. 325, Anglo-French conversations, 24 November 1938.

14 Quoted in Colvin, *Chamberlain Cabinet*, p. 182.

15 The House of Commons was "in a dreadful state about the partition of Czechoslovakia ... most people really believed that Munich settled the Czech question and are seriously disturbed" (H. Nicolson, *Diaries and Letters, 1930–1939* [paperback ed., London: Fontana, 1966], p. 385, diary entry, 14 March 1939).

16 House of Commons, *Parliamentary Debates*, 5th ser. (henceforth *Hansard*), vol. 345, col. 223, 14 March 1939.

17 *The Diplomatic Diaries of Oliver Harvey, 1937–1940*, ed. J. Harvey (London, 1970), pp. 261–62, diary entry, 14 March 1939.

18 *DBFP*, IV, no. 247, Halifax to Henderson, 14 March 1939.

19 PRO, Cab., 23/98, 15 March 1939.

20 *Hansard*, vol. 345, col. 440, 15 March 1939.

21 *DBFP*, IV, no. 279, Halifax to Henderson, 15 March 1939.

22 *Hansard*, vol. 345, col. 615, 16 March 1939.

23 *Times* (London), 17 March 1939.

24 The Earl of Birkenhead, *Halifax: The Life of Lord Halifax* (London, 1965), p. 432. Lord Birkenhead was at this time parliamentary private secretary to Lord Halifax.

25 *DBFP*, IV, no. 275, Shepherd to Halifax, 15 March 1939; no. 413n., Collier's minutes of visit by Lithuanian minister, 16 March 1939; no. 298, Sargent's minutes of visit by Rumanian ambassador, 16 March 1939.

26 Apparently, after a disagreement (A. C. Johnson, *Viscount Halifax: A Biography* [London, 1941], p. 514). On 16 March Henderson came out with a bitter denunciation of the invasion. Condemning its "utter immorality," he hoped that the British government would reconsider its attitude "towards a Government which has shown itself incapable of observing an agreement not six months old and which is apparently set on domination by force of the whole of the Danube basin" (*DBFP*, IV, no. 288, Henderson to Halifax, 16 March 1939).

27 *Times* (London), 18 March 1939.

28 Nicolson, *Diaries*, p. 386.

29 *DBFP*, IV, no. 395, Halifax to Hoare, 17 March 1939.

30 Harvey, *Diaries*, p. 263.

31 *DBFP*, IV, no. 394, Halifax to Lindsay, 17 March 1939.

32 *DBFP*, IV, no. 390, Halifax circular dispatch, 17 March 1939.

33 *DBFP*, IV, no. 399, Hoare to Halifax, 18 March 1939; no. 404, Phipps to Halifax, 18 March 1939; no. 418, Phipps to Cadogan, 18 March 1939.

34 Ibid.; no. 393, Phipps to Halifax, 17 March 1939; no. 398, Orde to Halifax, 18 March 1939.

35 Admiral Chatfield, for the Chiefs of Staff, told the Cabinet that German access to Rumanian oil fields would do much to nullify a British blockade. Political control, sure to follow, would be still more serious, since Germany could then move straight on

to the Mediterranean, relying on Bulgarian friendship. Little could be done, however, to help Rumania directly (Dilks, *Cadogan Diaries*, p. 160).

36 PRO, Cab., 23/98, 18 March 1939.

37 *DBFP*, IV, no. 446, Halifax to Phipps, Seeds, and Kennard, 20 March 1939. He went on to propose that the French, Polish, and Soviet governments join with His Majesty's Government in a declaration "to consult together as to what steps should be taken to offer joint resistance" to any action "which constitutes a threat to the political independence of any European state." Chamberlain personally appealed to Mussolini for some action to allay tension. Two days later, Lithuania ceded Memel to Germany. Chamberlain wished to mobilize the Air Defense of Great Britain and was "aghast" to learn that this would take twelve hours (Liddell Hart, *Memoirs*, II, 227). On 29 March he announced the doubling in size of the Territorial Army. On 31 March the guarantee of Poland was announced.

Chapter 7: Poland and the Corridor Crisis of March 1939

1 *PWB*, no. 10.

2 E.g., his reply to the German proposals of 24 October 1938 (*PWB*, no. 45, Beck to Lipski, 31 October 1938); his reply to Hitler of 5 January 1939 (*Documents on German Foreign Policy, 1918–1945*, Series D, V, [New York and London, 1953], no. 119, memorandum of conversation); and his instructions to Lipski of 25 March 1939 (*PWB*, no. 62).

3 R. Debicki, *Foreign Policy of Poland, 1919–1939* (London, 1963), p. 129. Szembek, the Polish under secretary of state for foreign affairs from 1933 to 1939, argued in November 1938 that "given the possibility of an armed conflict with Russia, Germany cannot risk compromising its good relations with us" (Comte J. Szembek, *Journal, 1933–1939* [Paris, 1952], p. 382). The Germans carefully fostered this illusion.

4 H. L. Roberts, "The Diplomacy of Colonel Beck," in *The Diplomats, 1919–1939*, ed. G. A. Craig and F. Gilbert (paperback ed., New York, Atheneum, 1971), pp. 583–84.

5 *PWB*, no. 44, Lipski to Beck, 25 October 1938.

6 *PWB*, no. 45, Beck to Lipski, 31 October 1938.

7 Szembek, *Journal*, p. 379, diary entry, 22 November 1938.

8 *Documents on German Foreign Policy*, V, no. 119, memorandum of conversation, 5 January 1939.

9 J. Beck, *Last Report* (New York, 1957), pp. 171–72; W. Jedrze-

jewicz, ed., *Diplomat in Berlin, 1933–1939: Papers and Memoirs of Jozef Lipski, Ambassador of Poland* (New York, 1968), p. 512 (henceforth *Lipski Papers*).

10 Szembek, *Journal*, pp. 413–15, diary entry, 1 February 1939.

11 G. Gafencu, *Last Days of Europe* (New Haven, 1948), pp. 40–41.

12 *FRUS 1939*, I, no. 14, Biddle to Secretary of State, 16 February 1939. Beck told Szembek that he attached "the greatest importance to maintaining good relations with Berlin" (Szembek, *Journal*, p. 426, diary entry, 8 February 1939).

13 Beck, *Last Report*, pp. 71–73.

14 *PWB*, no. 45, Beck to Lipski, 31 October 1938.

15 A. Polonsky, *Politics in Independent Poland, 1921–1939* (Oxford, 1972), pp. 375–76; H. Roos, *A History of Modern Poland* (London, 1966), pp. 154–56.

16 Szembek, *Journal*, pp. 356–58, diary entry, 18 October 1938.

17 *DBFP*, IV, no. 207, Kennard to Halifax, 11 March 1939.

18 *DBFP*, IV, no. 250, Kennard to Halifax, 14 March 1939.

19 L. B. Namier, *Diplomatic Prelude, 1938–1939* (London, 1948), p. 85.

20 *DBFP*, IV, no. 269, Kennard to Halifax, 15 March 1939.

21 *DBFP*, V, no. 6, Shepherd to Halifax, 4 April 1939.

22 Namier, *Diplomatic Prelude*, p. 85.

23 *DBFP*, IV, no. 498, report of British military attaché, 22 March 1939; report of U.S. military attaché, 20 March 1939, quoted in A. Toynbee and F. T. Ashton-Gwatkin, eds., *Survey of International Affairs, 1939–1946: The World in March 1939* (London: RIIA, 1952), p. 291.

24 *Sunday Times* (London), 19 March 1939.

25 Jedrzejewicz, *Lipski Papers*, pp. 499–500.

26 *Sunday Times* (London), 19 March 1939.

27 *FRUS 1939*, I, no. 49, Bullitt to Secretary of State, 17 March 1939; *Times* (London), 17 March 1939.

28 *DBFP*, IV, nos. 391 and 392, Kennard to Halifax, 17 March 1939.

29 *DBFP*, IV, no. 400, Kennard to Halifax, 18 March 1939.

30 *Times* (London), 20 March 1939; Jedrzejewicz, *Lipski Papers*, pp. 500–501.

31 *DBFP*, IV, no. 442, Kennard to Halifax, 20 March 1939; no. 471, Halifax to Kennard, 21 March 1939; no. 447, Kennard to Halifax, 20 March 1939.

32 *PWB*, no. 61, Lipski to Beck, 21 March 1939.

33 Szembek, *Journal*, pp. 432–34, diary entry, 22 March 1939.

34 *DBFP*, IV, no. 479, Kennard to Halifax, 22 March 1939.
35 *DBFP*, IV, no. 485, Kennard to Halifax, 22 March 1939.
36 Jedrzejewicz, *Lipski Papers*, p. 521.
37 *PWB*, no. 59; Szembek, *Journal*, pp. 432–33.
38 G. M. Gathorne-Hardy, *A Short History of International Affairs* (London, 1950), pp. 486–87.
39 Jedrzejewicz, *Lipski Papers*, p. 501n.; Roos, *Modern Poland*, p. 160; *DBFP*, V, no. 6, Shephard to Halifax, 4 April 1939.
40 *Times* (London), 25 March 1939; *DBFP*, IV, no. 515, Kennard to Halifax, 24 March 1939.
41 Szembek, *Journal*, p. 434, diary entry, 24 March 1939.
42 Jedrzejewicz, *Lipski Papers*, p. 504.

Chapter 8: The United States and the Straits Question, 1946

1 W. Hillman, *Mr. President* (New York, 1952), pp. 46–7.
2 *FRUS 1946*, VI, 696–707, Kennan to Byrnes, 22 February 1946.
3 W. S. Poole, "From Conciliation to Containment: The Joint Chiefs of Staff and the Coming of the Cold War, 1945–1946," *Military Affairs* 62 (February 1978): 14.
4 *FRUS 1946*, VII, 310.
5 *FRUS 1946*, VII, 346–47, memorandum, 16 August 1965.
6 H. Feis, *From Trust to Terror* (New York, 1971), p. 83.
7 *FRUS 1946*, VII, 802–3, H. N. Howard memorandum, 19 December 1945; pp. 1–3, Henderson memorandum, 28 December 1945.
8 *FRUS 1945*, VIII, 1265, U.S. note to Turkey, presented 2 November 1945.
9 H. Feis, *Between War and Peace* (Princeton, 1960), pp. 295–98.
10 *FRUS 1946*, VII, 901n; p. 820, quoted from a statement on Turkey (not included) of 27 February 1946.
11 Poole, "From Conciliation to Containment," p. 14.
12 *FRUS 1946*, VII, 822, Wilson to Byrnes, 12 April 1946.
13 Feis, *Between War and Peace*, p. 352.
14 Poole, "From Conciliation to Containment," p. 14.
15 *The Forrestal Diaries*, ed. W. Millis (New York, 1951), p. 143, diary entry, 10 March 1946. During the crisis itself Forrestal expressed his apprehension "about our capabilities to meet any sudden emergency in Europe" (ibid., p. 196, diary entry, 23 August 1946). Byrnes and Patterson (the secretary of war) both publicly expressed concern at the effects of demobilization (Department of State, *Bulletin*, XIV, 351, 24 March 1946; *New York Times*, 3 October 1946).

16 *New York Times*, 31 October 1946, quoting "official U.S. sources."
17 Montgomery of Alamein, *Memoirs* (London, 1958), p. 429.
18 Feis, *From Trust to Terror*, p. 183.
19 *FRUS 1946*, VI, 749, Smith to Byrnes, 28 April 1946.
20 *FRUS 1946*, VII, 829, Orekhov to Acheson, 7 August 1946.
21 J. M. Jones, *The Fifteen Weeks* (New York, 1955), pp. 62–63.
22 Poole, "From Conciliation to Containment," p. 15.
23 *FRUS 1946*, VII, 830–33, Jones memorandum, 9 August 1946.
    My emphasis.
24 Ibid., pp. 827n. and 836, Durbrow to Secretary of State, 12 August 1946.
25 Wilson had long warned of Soviet intentions against Turkey. As
    early as July 1945 he had described the situation as "menacing"
    (*FRUS 1946*, I, 1033–34).
26 *FRUS 1946*, VII, 836–37, Wilson to Secretary of State, 12 August
    1946.
27 *FRUS 1946*, VII, 840–41, Acheson to Byrnes, 15 August 1946.
28 Ibid., p. 840; *Forrestal Diaries*, p. 192.
29 D. Acheson, *Present at the Creation* (paperback ed., New York:
    Signet Books, 1969),p. 264.
30 *FRUS 1946*, VII, 847–48, Acheson to Orkhov, 19 August 1946.
31 Ibid., p. 852, Wilson to Secretary of State, 21 August 1946.
32 Ibid., pp. 894–96, memorandum on Turkey approved by Byrnes
    and Acheson, 21 October 1946.

Chapter 9: Clearing the Ground
 1 See G. Ryle, *The Concept of Mind* (London, 1949).
 2 "Perception", in *A Dictionary of the Social Sciences*, ed. J. Gould
    and W. L. Kolb (London, 1964), p. 491.
 3 J. Gosling, "Mental Causes and Fear," *Mind* 71 (1962): 297.
 4 R. Jervis, *Perception and Misperception in International Poli-
    tics* (Princeton, 1976), p. 147. Also see, among others, G. D.
    Paige, *The Korea Decision* (New York, 1968), p. 295.
 5 A contrary view is taken by Ernest May. He argues that admin-
    istration thinking about the Cold War took place "in a frame of
    reference made up in part of historical analogies, parallels, and
    presumed trends and that the history employed for this purpose
    was narrowly selected and subjected to no deliberate scrutiny
    or analysis." Yet the only documentary evidence adduced con-
    sists of two indirect and general quotations from the Forrestal
    diaries, which are quite insufficient, I believe, to prove a rather

one-sided case. See E. R. May, *Lessons of the Past* (New York, 1973), chap. 2, esp. pp. 33, 50–51.

6 R. S. Lazarus, *Psychological Stress and the Coping Process* (New York, 1966), p. 25. My emphasis.

7 Ibid., p. 44. My emphasis.

Chapter 10: Geopolitical Environment

1 D. G. Pruitt, "Definition of the Situation as a Determinant of International Action," in *International Behavior*, ed. H. G. Kelman (New York, 1965), pp. 400–401.

2 Quoted in C. W. Seton-Watson, *Italy from Liberalism to Fascism, 1870–1925* (London, 1967), p. 219.

3 W. L. Langer, *European Alliances and Alignments, 1871–1890* (New York, 1950), p. 472.

4 *PWB*, no. 45, Beck to Lipski, 3 October 1938.

5 *Un Livre Noir* (Paris, 1922–23), II, 363–73.

6 *DDF*, 3rd ser., IV, no. 311, Louis to Poincaré, 2 November 1912.

7 *GP*, XXXVIII, 206, Lucius to Foreign Office, 7 November 1913.

8 S. Sazonov, *Fateful Years: 1909–1916* (New York, 1928), p. 119.

9 D. Acheson, *Present at the Creation* (paperback ed., New York: Signet Books, 1969), p. 262.

10 *FRUS 1946*, VII, 809, Byrnes to Acheson, 18 January 1946.

11 Ibid., p. 823, Wilson to Acheson, 4 May 1946.

12 The term is used by O. R. Holsti, "Cognitive Dynamics and Images of the Enemy," in *Enemies in Politics*, ed. D. J. Finlay et al. (Chicago, 1967), p. 26.

13 See J. L. Gaddis, *The United States and the Origins of the Cold War, 1941–1947* (New York, 1972); D. S. McClellan, "Who Fathered Containment?" *International Studies Quarterly* 17, no. 2 (1973); G. Warner, "The Truman Doctrine and the Marshall Plan," *International Affairs* 50, no. 1 (1974).

14 H. Feis, *From Trust to Terror* (New York, 1971), p. 83.

15 Vicomte de Gontaut-Biron, *Mon ambassade en Allemagne, 1872–1873* (Paris, 1906), p. 105.

16 *DDF*, 1st ser., I, no. 308, Decazes circular dispatch, 17 July 1874.

17 PRO, FO, 27/2107/291, Lyons to Derby, 5 April 1875.

18 *Times* (London), 10 July 1889.

19 G. Giolitti, *Memoirs of My Life* (London, 1923), pp. 58–59.

20 A. N. Mandelstam, "La Politique russe d'accès à la Mediterranée au XXe siècle," *Académie de Droit Internationale, XXe Recueil des Cours* 47, no. 1 (1934): 635.

21 I. I. Astaf'ev, "Potsdamskoe Soglashenie 1911 g," *Istoricheskie Zapiski Akademii Nauk SSSR* 85 (1970).

22 I. I. Astaf'ev, "Voennaia trevoga v praviashchikh krugakh tsarskoi Rossii v oktiabre 1908 g," *Vestnik Moskovskogo Universiteta* 2 (1965).

23 *FRUS 1939*, I, 2–6, Halifax memorandum for Roosevelt, 24 January 1939.

24 *Times* (London), 7 February 1939.

25 Dilks, *Cadogan Diaries*, pp. 155–56.

26 PRO, Cab., 23/98, 15 March 1939.

27 Dilks, *Cadogan Diaries*, p. 161, entry for 20 March 1939. My emphasis.

28 R. Debicki, *Foreign Policy of Poland, 1919–1939* (London, 1963), p. 111.

29 *PWB*, no. 147, Lipski's "Final Report," Paris, 10 October 1939.

30 See Comte J. Szembek, *Journal, 1933–1939* (Paris, 1952), esp. pp. 379, 383–85.

31 G. Gafencu, *Last Days of Europe* (New Haven, 1948), p. 41.

32 R. S. Lazarus, *Psychological Stress and the Coping Process* (New York, 1966), p. 89.

33 U. Bialer, *The Shadow of the Bomber* (London: The Royal Historical Society, 1979).

34 J. Defrasne, "L'Armée française devant l'alerte de 1875," *Revue Historique de l'Armée* 26, no. 1 (1970).

35 PRO, FO, 27/2108/373, 1 May 1875.

36 C. Digeon, *La Crise allemande de la pensée française, 1870–1914* (Paris, 1959), p. 58.

37 See ibid.; also K. W. Swart, *The Sense of Decadence in Nineteenth-Century France* (The Hague, 1964), esp. pp. 122–38. For the effect of the obsession with invasion in public affairs, see E. M. Carroll, *French Public Opinion and Foreign Affairs, 1870–1914* (London, 1931).

38 PRO, FO, 27/2107/339, Adams to Derby, 26 April 1875.

39 Lord Newton, *Lord Lyons*, II (London, 1913), 54–57, 59.

40 Quoted in M. Howard, *The Continental Commitment* (paperback ed., London: Penguin, 1974), p. 124.

41 B. H. Liddell Hart, *Memoirs*, II (London, 1965), 227, diary note of conversation with Hore-Belisha, 27 March 1939.

42 P. Calvocoressi to the Editor of the *Times* (London), 1 August 1970. Also see P. Calvocoressi and G. Wint, *Total War* (paperback ed., London: Penguin, 1972), pp. 95–96.

43 Howard, *Continental Commitment*, p. 127.

44 Quoted in ibid., p. 113.

45 M. S. Anderson, *The Eastern Question* (London, 1966), p. 299.

46 *BD*, x, no. 382, O'Beirne to Grey, 27 November 1913.

47 Acheson, *Present at the Creation*, p. 262.

48 *The Forrestal Diaries*, ed. W. Millis (New York, 1951), p. 196, entries for 22 and 23 August 1946.

49 W. S. Poole, "From Conciliation to Containment: The Joint Chiefs of Staff and the Coming of the Cold War, 1945–1946," *Military Affairs* 62 (February 1978): 14.

50 *Akten zur deutschen auswärtigen Politik, 1918–1945*, Series D, VI (Baden-Baden, 1956), no. 115, Moltke to Foreign Office, 28 March 1939.

51 A. Polonsky, *Politics in Independent Poland* (Oxford, 1972), pp. 483–493.

52 M. Zgormiak, "Les Préparatifs allemands d'attaque contre la Pologne (1939) d'après les informations du Deuxième bureau d'état-major polonais," *Revue d'Histoire de la Deuxième Guerre Mondiale* 20 (1970): 53.

53 Polonsky, *Politics in Independent Poland*, pp. 478, 493, 500.

54 Jedrzejewicz, *Lipski Papers*, p. 504.

55 Zgormiak, "Les Préparatifs allemands," p. 42.

Chapter 11: Domestic Political Environment

1 C. Lockhart, *The Efficacy of Threats in International Interaction Strategies*, Sage International Studies Series 2 (1973); K. Knorr, "Threat Perception," in *Historical Dimensions of National Security Problems*, ed. K. Knorr (Lawrence, Kansas, 1976) pp. 78–119; J. Steinberg, "The Copenhagen Complex," *Journal of Contemporary History* 1 (1966): 23–46; D. G. Pruitt, "Definition of the Situation as a Determinant of International Action," in *International Behavior*, ed. H. G. Kelman (New York, 1965), pp. 393–432.

2 *Krasny Arkhiv* VI, 91 (Moscow, 1938), pp. 129–30, Orlov to Gorchakov, 26 April 1875.

3 N. R. Luttbeg, ed., *Public Opinion and Public Policy*, rev. ed. (Homewood, Ill., 1974), Introduction and p. 297.

4 PRO, FO, 45/624/161, Dering to Salisbury, 23 July 1889.

5 H. S. Zanansky, "Paranoid Reactions," in *International Encyclopedia of the Social Sciences* (New York, 1968). For a most informative discussion of the paranoid character see D. Shapiro, *Neurotic Styles* (New York, 1965), chap. 3.

6 G. Salvemini, *La politica estera di Francesco Crispi* (Rome, 1919), p. 11. The expression is derived from a letter written by

Crispi in 1877: "The history of this country teaches us that the unexpected is a monster to be feared."

7   W. J. Stillman, *Francesco Crispi* (London, 1899), pp. 7–8.

8   A. C. Jemolo, *Crispi* (Florence, 1922), p. 35.

9   Quoted in Stillman, *Francesco Crispi*, p. 18.

10 C. W. Seton-Watson, *Italy from Liberalism to Fascism, 1870– 1925* (London, 1967), p. 130; G. Pertico, "Governo e parlamento nella svolta del secolo," *Storia e Politica* 7 (1968).

11 I. L. Janis, *Victims of Groupthink* (New York, 1972).

12 *GP*, XXXVIII, 169, Wangenheim to Foreign Office, 3 December 1913: *Österreich-Ungarns Aussenpolitik von der Bosnischen krise 1908 bis zum kriegsausbruch 1914*, VII (Vienna and Leipzig, 1930), no 9054, Pallavicini to Foreign Office, 5 December 1913.

13 *BD*, X, no. 379, O'Beirne to Grey, 25 November 1913.

14 S. Sazonov, *Fateful Years: 1909–1916* (New York, 1928), p. 119.

15 *BD*, X, no. 380, O'Beirne to Grey, 26 November 1913; no. 443, Buchanan to Grey, 21 December 1913.

16 See Comte J. Szembek, *Journal, 1933–1939* (Paris, 1952), pp. 432–33, entry for 22 March 1939; *Times* (London), 18 March 1939; *Le Livre jaune français: Documents diplomatiques, 1938– 1939* (Paris, 1939), no. 75, Noël to Bonnet, 16 March, 1939; *Times* (London), 20 March 1939.

17 *Times* (London), 20 March 1939.

18 R. G. D. Laffan et al., *Survey of International Affairs, 1938*, III (London: RIIA, 1953), 290; H. L. Roberts, "The Diplomacy of Colonel Beck," in *The Diplomats, 1919–1939*, ed. G. A. Craig and F. Gilbert, II (paperback ed., New York: Atheneum, 1971), 580.

19 G. Gafencu, *Last Days of Europe* (New Haven, 1948), pp. 26– 27; L. Noël, *L'Aggression allemande contre la Pologne* (Paris, 1946), p. 22.

20 S. E. Asch, "Effects of Group Pressure upon the Modification and Distortion of Judgements," in *Basic Studies in Social Psychology*, ed. H. Proshansky and B. Seidenberg (New York, 1966).

21 Noël, *L'Aggression allemande*, p. 23; D. Cooper, *The Light of Common Day* (London, 1959), pp. 227–28.

22 Cooper, *The Light of Common Day*, pp. 227–28.

23 See A. Storr, "The Man," in A. J. P. Taylor et al., *Churchill: Four Faces and the Man* (paperback ed., London: Penguin, 1973), pp. 217–18.

24 J. Beck, *Last Report* (New York, 1957), pp. 13, 36, 90.

25 R. S. Lazarus, *Psychological Stress and the Coping Process* (New York, 1966), p. 133; S. B. Withey, "Sequential Accommodation to Threat," in *The Threat of Impending Disaster*, ed. G. H. Grosser et al. (Cambridge, Mass., 1964), p. 108.

26 L. Festinger, *A Theory of Cognitive Dissonance* (Evanston, Ill., 1957).

27 Gafencu, *Last Days*, pp. 44, 47.

28 *DBFP*, iv, no. 524, Kennard to Halifax, 25 March 1939.

29 Noël, *L'Aggression allemande*, p. 24.

30 W. R. Rock, *Appeasement on Trial* (Hamden, Conn., 1966), pp. 207–9.

31 H. Nicolson, *Diaries and Letters, 1930–1939* (paperback ed., London: Penguin, 1966), 392.

32 PRO, Cab., 23/98, 15 March 1939.

33 Nicolson, *Diaries*, 393.

34 *The Spectator*, 17 March 1939, p. 431.

35 The Earl of Birkenhead, *Halifax: The Life of Lord Halifax* (London, 1965), p. 432.

36 *Times* (London), 18 March 1939.

37 J. E. Wrench, *Geoffrey Dawson and Our Times* (London, 1955), p. 388.

38 K. Feiling, *Life of Neville Chamberlain* (London, 1946), p. 401.

39 For a review of the literature on this topic see W. J. McGuire, "The Nature of Attitudes and Attitude Change," in *The Handbook of Social Psychology*, ed. G. Lindzey and E. Aronson, iii (New York, 1968), 180, 237–40.

40 H. C. Kelman, "Compliance, Identification, and Internalization: Three Processes of Attitude Change," *Journal of Conflict Resolution* 2 (1958): 54.

41 S. Aster, *The Making of the Second World War* (London, 1973), pp. 227–28, 250, 253, 254–55.

42 Feiling, *Neville Chamberlain*, pp. 320–21, 372.

43 A. I. Gladstone and M. A. Taylor, "Threat-Related Attitudes and Reactions to Communications about International Events," *Journal of Conflict Resolution* 2 (1958): 26.

44 D. Katz, "The Functional Approach to the Study of Attitudes," *Public Opinion Quarterly* 24 (1960): 163–204.

45 S. Newman, *March 1939: The British Guarantee to Poland* (Oxford, 1976), p. 100.

46 A. A. Rogow, *James Forrestal* (New York, 1963).

Chapter 12: Appraisal: Structure

1 Lord Newton, *Lord Lyons*, II (London, 1913), 70–71, Lyons to Derby, 16 March 1875.

2 *DDF*, 1st ser., I, no. 369, Decazes to de Corcelle, 12 March 1875.

3 G. Hanotaux, *Contemporary France*, III (London, 1907), 252, Decazes to Gontaut-Biron, 14 May 1875.

4 *DDF*, 1st ser., I, no. 362, Decazes to de Jarnac, 6 March 1875; Hanotaux, *Contemporary France*, III, 212, Decazes to d'Harcourt, 9 April 1875; *DDF*, 1st ser., I, no. 428, Decazes circular dispatch, 18 May 1875.

5 R. Jervis, *Perception and Misperception in International Politics* (Princeton, 1976), p. 319.

6 G. Giolitti, *Memoirs of My Life* (London, 1923), p. 59.

7 *Materialy po franko-russikh otnoshenii za 1910–1914 gg* (Moscow, 1922), p. 633, Sazonov to Sverbeev, 10 November 1913.

8 A. N. Mandelstam, "La Politique russe d'accès à la Mediterranée au XXe siècle," *Académie de Droit International, Recueil des Cours*, 47, no. 1 (1934): 796.

9 *DBFP*, IV, nos. 391 and 392, Kennard to Halifax, 17 March 1939.

10 Ibid., no. 447, Kennard to Halifax, 20 March 1939.

11 *PWB*, no. 61, Lipski to Beck, 21 March 1939.

12 *FRUS 1939*, I, 102, Biddle to Cordell Hull, 29 March 1939.

13 *DBFP*, IV, no. 279, Halifax to Henderson, 15 March 1939.

14 Ibid.

15 Ibid., no. 394, Halifax to Lindsay, 17 March 1939.

16 *FRUS 1946*, VII, 840–42, Acheson to Byrnes, 15 August 1946; pp. 857–58, Joint Chiefs of Staff Memorandum, 23 August 1946.

17 Ibid., p. 802, memorandum, 19 December 1945.

18 J. D. Steinbruner, *The Cybernetic Theory of Decision* (Princeton, 1974).

Chapter 13: Appraisal: Theme

1 L. S. Stebbing, *Thinking to Some Purpose* (paperback ed., London: Penguin, 1939), pp. 30–31.

2 Duke de Broglie, *An Ambassador of the Vanquished* (London, 1896), p. 179.

3 G. Hanotaux, *Contemporary France*, III (London, 1907), 216, Decazes to de Noailles, 10 April 1875.

4 See, among others, W. L. Langer, *European Alliances and Alignments, 1871–1890* (New York, 1950), pp. 38–55; A. J. P. Taylor, *The Struggle for Mastery in Europe, 1848–1918* (London, 1954), pp. 225–27.

5 *DDF* 1st ser., I, no. 399, Decazes to Gontaut-Biron, 29 April 1875; A. Dreux, *Dernières années de L'ambassade en Allemagne de M. de Gontaut-Biron: 1874–1877* (Paris, 1907), pp. 98–99; Decazes to Gontaut-Biron, 29 April 1875.

6 *The Memoirs of Francesco Crispi*, ed. T. Palamenghi-Crispi, II (London, 1912), 393.

7 PRO, FO, 45/624/159, Dering to Salisbury, 23 July 1889.

8 B. von Siebert, *Graf Benckendorffs diplomatischer Schriftwechsel* (Berlin, 1928), III, 209, Sazonov to Benckendorff, 7 December 1913.

9 *BD*, IX, ii, no. 394, Grey to Cartwright, 18 December 1912: Siebert, *Benckendorffs diplomatischer Schriftwechsel*, II, 544, Benckendorff to Sazonov, 18 December 1912; *GP*, XXXIV, no. 57, Lichnowsky to Foreign Office, 18 December 1912.

10 *BD*, X, i, no. 174, Mallet to Grey, 17 December 1913.

11 *Materialy po franko-russikh otnoshenii za 1910–1914 gg* (Moscow, 1922), p. 633, Sazonov to Sverbeev, 10 November 1913.

12 PRO, Cab., 23/98, 15 March 1939.

13 *DBFP*, III, no. 288, Henderson to Halifax, 16 March 1939.

14 *DBFP*, IV, no. 279, Halifax to Henderson, 15 March 1939.

15 *Times* (London), 18 March 1939.

16 B. H. Liddell Hart, *Memoirs*, II (London, 1965), 219, diary entry, 16 March 1939.

17 *PWB*, no. 147, Lipski's "Final Report," 10 October 1939.

18 Jedrzejewicz, *Lipski Papers*, pp. 499–500.

19 *PWB*, no. 61, Lipski to Beck, 21 March 1939.

20 Jedrzejewicz, *Lipski Papers*, pp. 384–85, Lipski to Beck, 24 August 1938.

21 Comte J. Szembek, *Journal, 1933–1939* (Paris, 1952), p. 434, diary entry, 24 March 1939.

22 *FRUS 1946*, VII, 847, Acheson to Orekhov, 19 August 1946.

23 Ibid., p. 836, Wilson to Acheson, 12 August 1946.

24 Ibid., p. 848, Acheson to Orekhov, 19 August 1946.

25 *The Forrestal Diaries*, ed. W. Millis (New York, 1951), p. 192, diary entry for 15 August 1946.

Chapter 14: "Rules" of International Conduct

1 T. Parsons, "Order and Community in the International Social System," *International Politics and Foreign Policy*, ed. J. N. Rosenau, 1st ed. (New York, 1961), p. 120.

2 Ibid., p. 121.

3 K. J. Holsti, *International Politics*, 2nd ed. (Englewood Cliffs, N.J., 1972), pp. 64–66, 178–80. See also pp. 83–85.
4 M. A. Kaplan, *System and Process in International Politics* (New York, 1957).
5 E. McWhinney, *"Peaceful Coexistence" and Soviet-Western International Law* (Leyden, 1964), pp. 181–94.
6 D. K. Lewis, *Convention: A Philosophical Study* (Cambridge, Mass., 1969).
7 M. S. Quinn, "Practice-Defining Rules," *Ethics* 86 (October 1975): 76–86.
8 T. C. Schelling, *The Strategy of Conflict* (Cambridge, Mass., 1960), chap. 3.
9 Ibid., p. 259.
10 Jedrzejewicz, *Lipski Papers*, pp. 503–4, memorandum of conference, 24 March 1939. My emphasis.

Index

DESIGNED BY TED SMITH/GRAPHICS
COMPOSED BY GRAPHIC COMPOSITION, INC., ATHENS, GEORGIA
MANUFACTURED BY THOMSON-SHORE, INC., DEXTER, MICHIGAN
TEXT AND DISPLAY LINES SET IN CALEDONIA

Library of Congress Cataloging in Publication Data
Cohen, Raymond, 1947–
Threat perception in international crisis.
Includes bibliographical references and index.
1. International relations—Research.   2. World politics—19th century.
3. World politics—1900–1945.   I. Title.
JX1291.C53   327′.11   79–3964
ISBN 0–299–08000–5